Shipping Container Homes

Building a Home Using Containers – A Simple How to Guide for Beginners

Contents

Introduction

There comes a point in everyone's life when they have to move out of their parents' place and get one of their own. It is a natural part of evolution and the growth journey of an individual – and an essential one that makes a lot of difference in what kind of person you grow up to be. The timing for this differs from one case to another, and from one place to another, but it is an inevitable step.

Nowadays, unfortunately, getting a place of your own is easier said than done. Most young people find themselves stuck in rentals for years because the average house price in a place like the United States, for example, is over a quarter of a million dollars, which is not within many people's budgets. Being a homeowner has become a dream that many aspire to, but few reach at a reasonable age. Work multiple jobs, and you might afford a mortgage when you're 40, which is definitely not what any person wants. Yet, there are other ways.

Don't work three jobs for 15 years to afford your dream home; you can make it yourself. This home is also ideal for someone with money and wants to experiment with a vacation home or another property elsewhere. You can build yourself a shipping container home wherever you want, and it won't cost you as much money as buying a traditional house.

Shipping container homes have been rising in popularity over the years, and for good reason. This book will explore the question, what in God's name is a shipping container home? Everything you need to know about this modern-day invention will be outlined, including the cost of getting a shipping container home, how to set it up, how to furnish it, the permits you need for such a place, and much more.

What Is a Shipping Container Home?

As the name implies, it is a habitat made out of a shipping container. Since their inception in the 50s, shipping containers have revolutionized the transportation industry, making it possible to transport large amounts of goods in capable vessels. It took a few decades, but they were then used as a living space, and they are also making waves in the residential and real estate world.

You can make a 100-square foot of floor space home from just one small container. Eight containers can make you a two-story, 1400-square feet home, and so on. This is why they have been rising in popularity as a habitat for people with the space to fit them and the dedication to turn those steel containers into habitable houses that are both elegant and functional, and most important, affordable. This brings us to a fundamental question.

Why Invest in a Shipping Container Home?

You Can Start from Scratch

Unlike traditional real estate, with shipping container homes, you can start from scratch. There is the option to order a prefab home, but you can handle every detail yourself; the choice is yours. This gives you the freedom to start the design process from the very basics to the lamps you want to use, which brings us to the next point.

Easy Customization

One of the biggest perks of shipping container homes is that they are easily customizable. Whatever it is you've dreamed of having in your dream home, you can do it to a shipping container home and with style, too. The little details that people often are forced to neglect or accept in traditional houses can be addressed in shipping container homes, and you can customize it however you like. This is because making a home out of a shipping container is easy and you can execute the design you have in mind without many complications.

Many Companies Are Doing It Now

Another huge bonus to shipping container homes is that a lot of companies are offering services to such homes now. You don't have to worry about doing it all yourself or having to find a contractor that can do it. Owing to their immense popularity now, and the fact that there are millions of surplus containers in the country, several companies have entered that business, offering excellent services to help homeowners make their dream homes, so you won't be alone on this journey.

Affordable

This is perhaps the biggest reason shipping container homes are popular now. You can get a furnished and habitable house for a fraction of what it would cost to get a traditional home. As we mentioned earlier, an average house can cost you hundreds of thousands of dollars, and it might not even be to your liking, but rather a budget choice. While you can splurge on your shipping container home, getting numerous containers, adding a ton of modifications, and even enlisting the help of professional contractors, it would still be significantly cheaper than getting a traditional home in the cheapest part of your city.

Predictable Costs

Building a traditional house is often full of surprises. Unexpected costs emerge, from expensive tiles to required touches and finishes you didn't see coming. With shipping container homes, that is not the case. Most of the cost is predictable. The majority of the work on a container happens in the factory, and this is for a fixed price. Then you have the additional costs of delivery to the site of your home, laying the foundation, assembly, and other costs like utility connections and flooring. These, too, can be easily gauged beforehand, so you'll most likely know what you're walking into.

Quick to Build

The average house takes months to be properly built, but a shipping container home could be finished within a few weeks. This is another advantage that many people are coming to appreciate, especially those with already complex living situations who can't afford to stay without a home for much longer. When you build a new home, excitement and anticipation can be too much to handle; the last thing you need is waiting for the better part of a year to move in. Moreover, shipping container homes save you money as well, because longer durations mean more workers getting paid and more resources being spent. The less time the property takes, the more money you save.

If you order a prefab container home, you probably will get it even faster than if you got the containers and did it yourself. A lot of companies offer prefab options now, and you get to choose from the many available models.

Legal

Some people worry that shipping container homes might not be legal or up to standard building codes, but they are. A shipping container is designed to withstand a lot of weight and wear, so they meet most building codes out there; it's unlikely they would be illegal in your area. You just need to get the right permits (which we'll discuss later in the book) and you'll be good to go.

Sustainable

One of the biggest and most relevant advantages to a shipping container home is that they are sustainable and environmentally friendly. We live in a world plagued by not one, but *many* environmental crises, and the sustainability of your new place should be something you consider, if not for you then for your children. Shipping containers serve that end goal perfectly. The average container is made out of 85% recycled steel, which, alone, is one of the most sustainable aspects of this structure. So, as soon as you get one, you're already helping the environment.

Stats show that excess shipping containers in the US and the world are numbered in the hundreds of millions, so there is no need to have new ones manufactured. You're reusing something that was already built for a different purpose, which is one of the core practices of sustainability. Now, compare these recycled steel containers with cement, concrete, bricks, and wood, and you will find they are a much better option for the environment, and they have minimal impact compared to those other elements.

Durable

As we mentioned earlier, shipping containers are strong and can withstand wear and tear for many years. The average container holds over 26 tons of weight, so you don't need to worry about their strength. The steel they are designed from can take whatever you throw at it, which is why—believe it or not—shipping containers are often used as emergency shelters during natural disasters like earthquakes, hurricanes, or wars. This means you need not worry about your shipping container home blowing in the wind or crumbling under heavy rain. It is there to stay, and it can last you many years if you properly maintain it.

Speaking of rain, those containers are also designed to be watertight because the goods transported might be ruined if they get wet. True, you will modify the container to make it your home, but with the right techniques, you can still retain that quality and keep your container home safe from outside conditions.

Easily Moved

You already know that a shipping container can be moved or stacked however you like, which is great because you can get a few and build your home with ease. You can also move your shipping container home after it has been built, disassembling it and moving it with the right help. It is definitely difficult and it will need a lot of consideration, but it can be done. You can't do the same with a traditional house—how do you expect to lift a wooden house from its foundations?

Now that you know the advantages of getting a shipping container home, you need to consider several other angles. Where do you start?

Chapter 1: Starting Out

Choosing a Location

If you already have a piece of land you want to use for your shipping container home, then you not might need to delve deeper into this part. However, you have to be certain that your land qualifies to accommodate the shipping containers and your design will work there; , if not, you might just have to find an alternative. You will also need to be certain that zoning regulations and building codes allow you to build a shipping container home in that area. If you don't have land, there are certain factors you need to consider.

Budget

You need to set a budget for the land you will buy for your home. Finding land is already complicated and you don't want to worry about the design of your container home just yet; the time for that will come later. For now, just pour your efforts into finding land that works within your budget, without jeopardizing the money you want to invest in the home itself. Divide your budget into two portions, one for the land and one for the container home.

Experts recommend, though, that if you have a considerable budget, then you should design the container home first, and then find a piece of land that can accommodate your design. This will help you find a piece of land sure to work with your design in mind. It won't be easy, but it is worth the trouble and will save you time and effort. So, what other factors should you remember while looking for land?

The General Area

When buying a traditional house, you consider the neighborhood. Are there schools nearby? Where's the nearest hospital? Is it safe for you and your family? Does it have trees? Think of this as a regular house purchase, not a shipping container home. Consider the location of the land from all possible aspects so you can be 100% certain this is an area you would like to live in. Yes, you have a budget for the land, but that doesn't mean you should settle for any location. If your shipping home isn't perfect in terms of location, not just the design, then you should delay the construction until you find the best location.

An important factor related to the area is how close the land is to the main road. A lot of shipping container homeowners like to dwell in rural areas or locations where there aren't many buildings, and that might entail challenges. You need your land to be close to a main road just in case anything happens, and check that there is easy access there so you can make your way out easily in the case of emergencies.

Size

Assuming you like the neighborhood, you then need to consider the size of the land. There are different schools of thought here. The first suggests that you should design your shipping container home first – if even theoretically – or at least look at prefab models, and after that, try to find a piece of land that can accommodate your design. The second approach is finding a piece of land that works within your budget and then design your container home to fit within that land. Both approaches will work, but which will work best for your case should be decided only by you.

Do the math and figure out which approach works best for you. At the end of the day, you want a piece of land just the right size to accommodate your shipping container home. You don't need it to be too big, but it definitely can't be too small, or else this whole project could go awry.

Water Access

Another very important factor you need to think about is water access in the land you're thinking of buying. How would you supply your house with water? Is there a well nearby or a river? Or do you get water from another source? These questions are important in rural areas. The last thing you need is to purchase a piece of land only to discover later that it is rather difficult to supply your home with any water because there aren't any nearby sources.

Type of Soil

Building a shipping container home on sandy soil would not be a good idea. You have to understand about the soil in which the land exists, so it poses no risk to the home you want to construct. It might be a good idea to consult with experts here after having a soil sample checked. Unless you understand soil, you need someone with the necessary knowledge to guide you on this one.

Are You the Only Nonstandard Building?

If you find a piece of land that fits the description and seems excellent for what you have in mind, inspect the area in search of other nonstandard buildings like other shipping container homes, sheds, cabins, and fixed trailers. This will show you how easy it might be to get a permit, because if they can do it, then so can you. Finding unconventional buildings like that indicates how open the zoning is in an area.

How to Select the Right Shipping Container

Not all shipping containers are alike, and you have to examine the ones you're about to get for your home. These are some factors that you have to consider while looking for a shipping container.

1. Grades and Condition

There are different grades and conditions of shipping containers, and you have to understand the specifics because you will be choosing from those categories and using the container as your home. This knowledge is common to people who work in the cargo and shipping world, but the quality and structural integrity of your container home will depend on your choice of grade; educate yourself on this! Shipping containers are generally divided into two main categories: new and used. Just because it is used, it doesn't mean it is of bad quality, and vice versa. You will need to do further inspections either way, so you find the best option for your home.

One-trip container: As the name implies, these were manufactured, loaded with one cargo, and then shipped to their destination and sold without further usage. These are technically considered new containers because they experienced little wear or many trips on the road/water, and they are often in excellent condition. You will need to pay a bit extra for those, but it is worth the price because you'll be getting a container in a very good shape or "as good as new," as experts say.

Refurbished: Refurbished containers are another example of "as good as new," but there isn't an industry standard as to what might be called *refurbished,* so you will have to ask around to understand what exactly that means in this container's case. You will ask the seller what steps they followed in refurbishing said containers, and whether it complies with industry safety standards (ask for proof of that compliance so you can be 100% certain that it is safe).

New: These containers have never been used to transport cargo and should be in excellent condition. A new container is manufactured so you get it directly from the factory, though it will still need to have the proper certification when shipped to you, as it has to comply with safety standards and regulations. Pro tip: the outside of a new shipping container might show wear and tear since it will still be handled at ports for shipping, but the inside should be in mint condition since it has never been used to transport cargo.

Used: This is a bit of a different story with used containers because you can't know how long it has been used for. This term includes any container from those that have been used twice to those who have seen years of service. If you are getting a used container, you need to be certain that it is in good condition and hasn't suffered significant wear and tear beyond repair, because this might jeopardize its structural integrity. A few categories fall under the "used container" umbrella.

Cargo Worthy (CW)

If a used container meets the required requirements and has the necessary certification, it will be deemed cargo worthy, meaning it is fit to haul cargo. There, you might consider such a shipping container for your home since it will perform up to the standard of a new container in terms of carrying loads.

Wind and Water-Tight (WWT)

This is another phase in a shipping container's life cycle that you should understand. There are few, if any, differences between cargo-worthy (CW) and wind and watertight (WWT) containers – at least, not for the untrained eye. The WWT container is generally considered to be in a shape slightly worse than CW containers, aesthetically at least. It might have a few more scratches or dents, depending on what the condition. WWT containers are still considered very functional and in excellent shape, and they're also very economical, which is why you might want to consider them for your container home. The great thing is that they can even be further improved with minor repair work.

As-Is Containers

This is the final phase of a shipping container's life cycle, and it means you have no guarantees with this one. It will not live up to CW and WWT standards, and cannot expect the same functions from this type. As-is containers often have pretty noticeable damage, which is one reason why they can't be classified as **WWT**. They are most likely too old to fit into a higher category, even with repairs. If you are considering getting a container from this category, you need to always assume the worst. Have it inspected thoroughly, and visit the container to see it for yourself and ask about the specification and any compliance issues with this container.

So, what is the better option? A lot of factors come into play, beginning with your budget. Many experts claim that one-trip containers might be the best choice because they have been used for just the single cargo carried toward its final destination. One-trip and new containers are often used interchangeably. The advantage of getting a one-trip container is you will have a nice discount compared to a new one, which certainly helps.

Refurbished containers undergo an outside renovation process, mostly, to improve their aesthetic value. So, they remove dents, scratches, or any other problems from surface of the container to make it look more appealing to potential buyers. It will mostly depend on the local seller because they often handle the refurbishment aspect of the business; this may serve to improve the quality of the container. This is unlike repaired containers, which undergo repairs and will most likely have spare parts added. Those might look a bit ugly, but they mostly comply with safety and manufacturing standards, and they get the job done.

As for CW and WWT containers, they are also good options to consider since they pass the certification and quality tests, and they are durable, though they might be in a worse shape than the previous options. This is because they are *used* containers, unlike the new or newish options mentioned earlier. As for as-is containers, this is an option you should be careful with because they will most likely not be very reliable. In this next table, we will explore the pros and cons of these options.

	New/one-trip/refurbished	Cargo-worthy	Wind and watertight	As-is
Condition	Mint or near-mint condition, fresh paint, with no or minimal scratches and dents	Good condition, with some scratches and dents, and possible surface rust. Faded paint	Acceptable condition, a lot of scratches and dents, and faded paint	Usable but not very good condition. Many dents, scratches, and possible holes in the floor. Faded paint
Wind and watertight	Yes	Yes	Yes	Not guaranteed
Functioning doors	Yes	Yes	Yes	Not guaranteed
Easily modified	Yes	Yes	Yes	Will need repairs
Floor holes	No	No	No	Not guaranteed

Advantages	1. **Easy to modify** This container is much easier to modify than all the rest because there are minimal scratches and no dents, so nothing will interfere with your modifications. 2. **Minimal repairs required** Another great feature to newish containers is how they look, and the fact that they require minimal repairs, if any. Everything works—floors are in good condition, the roof provides the necessary protection, and so on.	1. **More available** One of the biggest advantages to used containers, whether that is CW or WWT, is that they are easily available. It doesn't matter where you live in the world, you probably can easily find used containers somewhere around you, which isn't as easily done with new or one-trip containers. This means you won't have to suffer a long search to find a used container, and you can work on your house early on. 2. **Cheaper** The main reason people resort to used shipping containers is that they are likely to be more affordable compared to newer ones. The quality will be the deciding factor in how big the difference in pricing will be, but a used container will always be cheaper.	As-is containers are used, so they have the same advantages of the CW or WWT containers, but they come with more flaws.

3. More durable

Because these containers at an earlier stage of their life cycle, they will live longer. They are more durable, and you are guaranteed a longer lifespan since they still have many years ahead of them.

4. Safer

With newer containers, you don't have to worry about the history of the container or what it might have gone through like transporting toxic materials or having a hidden flaw.

3. Better for the environment

While the concept of shipping containers, in general, is better for the environment, when you're using used containers, you're providing a bigger service to mother nature. You're reusing a steel container, without asking a factory to produce a new one for you, which is certainly better for the environment. You'll be basically using a container otherwise stored with no use.

Disadvantages	More expensive than other available options	Used shipping containers aren't as pristine as newish ones, which will show, aesthetically speaking. More important, it might make it more complicated to change your containers since there might be a dent here or a bump there that would require repairs first before you can get to work on the container. You also might not have a clear history of a shipping container that might have been used for a long time, so it might have transported dangerous materials you wouldn't want in your container home.		There are no guarantees with as-is containers, so you'll be rolling the dice. You might find one in a relatively acceptable condition that can be repaired to become livable, but that is not a sure thing and you might face expected complications.
Verdict	Best condition	Good, meets requirements	Suitable for storage, can't be used for shipping	Nothing is guaranteed

2. CSC Certification

We mentioned the word "certification" a few times now, but what type are we talking about? You need to understand these details because you must check the container you are about to buy to make sure that it is CSC certified. Inspecting containers happens regularly since they have to meet safety standards. The most important of those inspections is the International Convention for Safe Containers (CSC) check that gives containers the certification to show they can be transported and load cargos.

In the 70s, the CSC decided that containers need a system of maintenance and regular checks, repairs, and inspections so they can live up to a certain standard and ensure the safety of everyone involved in their handling, from the public to cargo loaders. So, how can you know if the container is CSC-compliant? You will check the data plate mounted in front of a container with all the necessary data. This CSC plate will have all the information you need to know about the container, like the owner (BIC code), and more important, a CSC safety approval.

3. Decals

While a decal is a harmless sticker that can be easily removed from your shipping container, it is what the decal signifies that is crucial. As we hinted earlier, some used shipping containers might have been transporting hazardous materials when they were in service -something you need to be mindful of. These hazardous materials might have leaked onto the floors or walls of the container, which might be problematic. Fortunately, companies selling containers have to mark such containers with decals indicating that they were used to transport possibly toxic substances.

While that is reassuring, you never know if there was something wrong with the records or if it was used to transport such materials before being used to move other less hazardous stuff. So, it's worth checking the history of the container and inquiring about any such occurrences. Even if the container was used to transport dangerous chemicals, it is a problem that can be overcome, but you need to know that fact so you can address the problem.

4. Size

There are different sizes for shipping containers, but know the basic or standard unit measurements at least. The most common lengths are 20 and 40 ft containers, with the 20 being the most versatile and readily available one. A 20-foot container offers around 160 square feet of space, while the 40 ft. offers twice as much space at 320 square feet.

Then you have high cube containers, which are taller than a standard shipping container. They are often taller by one foot. Though they come in the same lengths, high cube containers offer a bigger volume because of that extra foot of height, increasing their overall size. This is why high cube containers are most commonly used in shipping container homes as they offer a more spacious feeling. This extra ceiling height has made them very popular considering that that one foot does help people feel less claustrophobic compared to a standard container without the additional height.

So, which of these should you go for? That will depend on a variety of factors, starting with your design. If the design involves high ceilings, the high cube container is the best option. Conversely, if the height of the ceiling doesn't factor into your design, but length does, then you opt for a 40-foot standard container. You will also want to know if the container you have in mind can be stacked—it will most likely be possible because shipping containers are designed with stacking options of up to 9 containers; still, always ask.

5. Cost

The last factor that will play into the shipping container you choose is cost. Budgeting is everything when it comes to buying a container for your home because this is just the tip of the iceberg. You still have a lot of costs to cover, and you have to make sure you're within your budget.

Note: these numbers are averages; they might be slightly cheaper or more expensive than that at your local vendor.

	Newish (one-trip)	Used
Container type		
Standard 20 foot	$3,000	$2,100
Standard 40 foot	$5,600	$2900
High cube 20 foot	$3,300	$2,300
High cube 40 foot	$6,000	$3,000

Getting a new container will be more expensive than a one-trip one. However, as you might have noticed, the difference between the used container and a newish one isn't that much, so that's something you need to remember and decide (according to your budget) whether you'd like higher quality for that difference or not.

How to Inspect a Container

If you've checked all the above points and have found a couple of shipping containers you like, you still need to check them out first before you buy any. The inspection of a shipping container isn't complicated, but you have to do it in an orderly fashion so you can ensure that you have covered all your bases. These tips will help you make sure that no unexpected problems will pop up with the shipping containers after you've bought them.

1. See for yourself

One of the best things you can do for yourself and your future shipping container home is to go see the containers in person. If there is a local vendor you can drive to, do it. Don't take the shortcut and settle for pictures or videos, because those might not always show everything, and you might still face unexpected problems that were not shown in the footage. If driving to the vendor yourself is not an option, then ask them to film specific parts of the container—which we will discuss later —so you can make sure that all the usual problems aren't there. Never settle for prerecorded videos or photos since they might not show the critical angles you need to see.

2. Examine structural integrity

While there are other specifics to a sturdy shipping container you will also have to inspect, nothing is more important than the steel's structural integrity. If this is compromised, it could be dangerous to the home and everyone living in it. A shipping container is supported by 12 steel beams, which give it the structural strength it needs to carry such intense loads. Those beams, which form the edges of the six faces of a container, need to be in excellent condition and un-compromised. You can't take those beams out for inspection, so a surface examination must do; still, it needs to be *thorough*.

Surface rust isn't something that you should be worried about, but if that rust runs deep into the body of the beam and comes with corrosion, then this might be a faulty container with compromised structural integrity.

3. Doors

End doors are the only mechanical part of the container, which puts them at great jeopardy of suffering from rust or corrosion, as well as other joint problems that might render the door useless. You need to check the doors thoroughly when you inspect the container to ensure that the doors open around the hinges smoothly and that it locks properly. Make sure there aren't any missing parts around the door because those will need to be replaced or else your door might get damaged.

4. Container underside

Most people will neglect to check the underside of the container, assuming it is not important, but it offers the main support for the container itself to carry the loads in/on it. The underside comprises transverse beams that are the width of the container wide, and the plywood floor of the container is screwed into those cross beams. You will need to inspect those beams as well to make sure that they are in good shape and there aren't any complications.

It is crucial that you look for rust there since those beams are the most exposed to moisture and out of the sun's reach, so if it's a used container, you will definitely find rust. The question is, how bad is it? The good news is you can fix any damage down there, though it has to be caught early on or else it might cause problems down the line. Pro tip: be very careful when examining the underside of a container. Never stand or lay directly under it; use a camera or other photography tools instead.

5. Roof

Now that you've checked the base of the container, it is time to check the roof. It is often made out of corrugated metal, and it will look a different compared to the walls. You should be able to climb on top of the container to have a good look at the roof and make sure that it's acceptable. Look for dents and scratches that might run too deep. Make sure that any existing rust is just on the surface and hasn't seeped into the structure of the steel since that will be problematic. You also should check if the roof is waterproof, but you need to do the interior inspection first before doing that. Pro tip: if you're planning on putting another container over this one, then most of these checks won't be needed since the roof will be covered anyway. Don't waste your time doing checks and inspections that will prove useless once your container home is finished.

6. Walls

In terms of appearance, the walls might just be the most important part of the container because this makes up most of what people see when they look at a shipping container. So, you need to consider this while shopping for one. Both the side and end walls of the container are made of corrugated steel responsible for their structural strength. Check the walls for rust like you did with other parts of the container, and if it is there, make sure it's just on the surface. Any problems digging deep into the walls might be problematic, and a hole is *definitely* a big problem.

You can fix a hole, but it won't be the last one headed your way if the walls are already in that state. To know if the walls have rooted rust, use a hammer to tap into the area in doubt. If large pieces of steel fall off, then the structural integrity of the walls are compromised. Dents in the walls can also be quite annoying and might hinder your plans. If the dent is on the outside, you might not be able to put an adjoining container beside it. If dents are on the inside, they might interfere with your design for the interior of the container. This is why you have to make sure that the dents, if any, are small and won't be a nuisance once you start the construction of your home.

7. Interiors and floors

After finishing with the exterior and floors of your container, you need to move to the inside in the same way. The inside walls need to be in good shape with no serious rust or dents, and the structural frame and its beams have to be solid with no bends or other visible problems. There's a very effective test you can perform to check if any leaks might jeopardize the water tightness of the container. Close the container as best as you can with you on the inside, and look for any light seeping into the dark container while you are there. If there is any, then there is a high probability that the container isn't waterproof and will need repairs and patching to fix that. This test obviously has to be done during the day so you can see if any light sneaks inside.

Last but not least, the floors need to be thoroughly inspected because those are basically as important as the floors of a traditional house. Shipping containers have different flooring types, but the most common is plywood. Why is it crucial that you pay special attention to the floors? Well, they can absorb materials since this is the only part of the container with permeability. As we mentioned earlier, you have no idea what was transported in the container a few months earlier, and it might just be chemicals. So, close the doors for a while and then step inside and do a smell test. If you smell chemicals or mold, then there is a problem with the floors. Maybe it just absorbed the chemical, but it also might mean there is a leak in the floor. In any case, make sure the smell isn't too strong. It might not be a major problem, but if you have options to choose from, stay away from the containers that smell funky on the inside; that smell might indicate mold or chemicals.

With this thorough inspection, along with the CSC plate mentioned earlier that provides a detailed history of the container, you should have a good idea of what state the container is in and whether you should move forward with the purchase.

What container should you get?

We have been talking for quite a while about the different types of containers and the pros/cons of each, the factors affecting your choice, and how to properly inspect a shipping container. With those points in mind and a budget, your choices should be somewhat narrower, and you can answer the question of which container you should purchase. Knowing all this, should you just purchase any container that fits the description and is in good condition? Not before answering these following questions.

Question	Pointers
1. Do you care about container appearance and aesthetics?	If so, then you should go for a newish container—either new or one-trip; otherwise, you will spend time modifying an older one to make it look better.
2. Is there a chance you might move your container home?	Here, go for cargo-worthy containers since those can handle the move without compromising the loads or the structural integrity of your house.
3. Will you remove large chunks of the walls to create bigger open spaces?	Then the container walls need to be in excellent condition, and you have to thoroughly check the structural integrity of the main support beams to make sure you won't compromise the remaining walls.
4. Will you change the floors either way?	There, damage to the existing plywood floors is insignificant since you will be replacing it or adding a finished floor over it.

5. Are you adding a separate roof?	In this case, any damage to the container roof shouldn't worry you because it won't matter.
6. Will you be using several containers?	If you are, it is always advisable to buy them all from the same shipping line to make sure there are minimal differences in measurements or conditions, which will make it easier for you to stack several containers and build a home with more than one container.

Now, you should know everything you need to know before you purchase shipping containers to build your home. This might seem like a lot, but this is arguably the most important step of the entire construction process. If you get the right containers, then what follows will be easier and smoother. So, take your time with this step and get it right.

Permits

You can't just buy a couple of containers and then put them on your land as a home. If you will build a residential structure, you need first to check the zoning laws in your area to make sure that it is legal to build the structure you want to build. After that, you have to get the necessary permits so you can be 100% certain that zoning or regulations are met. Getting the right containers for your home is just the first phase of this project, and there are a few more before you finally have a shipping container home. In this upcoming section, we will explore the type of permits you might have to get to build such a home, and provide examples of zoning laws that might make it difficult for you to move forward.

Factors Affecting the Legality of a Shipping Container Home

Getting the necessary permit for a shipping container home isn't as simple as just applying for one. In some countries, they will appoint a city building inspector to come and view the location and the structure to make sure everything is legal. There are factors that they must clear before you can get your permit.

Location safety: Their first major concern is about safety. There are certain things they will inspect to make sure that the property poses no risk to its inhabitants or anyone else in the surrounding areas. With the land, this means they might inspect the soil to verify the surface stability and make sure that the ground will not collapse under heavy loads. They will also check for any risks of uplift or overturning.

Structural safety: Next, they will check your structure to make sure it is in a good shape and is at no risk of collapsing. They will look for proper anchorage and wind resistance, and any other factors that might compromise the structural safety of the shipping container home.

Building regulations

Shipping containers share the same requirements and regulations imposed on regular buildings in most countries. This means they have to be zoned properly and follow the regulations set forth by the city just like any other construction. These are some regulations that you might have to clear, depending on where you are in the world.

1. Property Zoning

You've probably come across the term "zoning" quite a few times, but what does it mean? Zoning is when a city divides different, large pieces of land into zones or sections that can accommodate certain types of structures. It's often the city's responsibility to handle zoning since it is their way of determining how the city's growth can move forward and the development plans for a certain location. It's also a way of grouping similar buildings together and thus control the density or the distribution of certain structures. For instance, zoning determines which parts of the city will be allocated for commercial buildings, and what other areas will be residential neighborhoods.

2. Building Codes

To build any structure, there are certain codes you have to follow to ensure that certain standards of construction are upheld. Residential houses have a set of codes, as do office buildings or high-rises and just about any structure out there. A shipping container home is one of those structures, so you will need to apply for the relevant building permits to prove that your property complies with the relevant building codes. These codes are sometimes based on international versions that set the standard for things like electricity, plumbing, and fire protection, which is why they have to be followed.

3. Mobile, modular, and manufactured building codes

Shipping container homes aren't your standard home, so different codes might apply to them, and you need to identify those so you can comply with them. The problem is, discovering the difference between mobile, modular, and manufactured homes can be a bit tricky, so you need to understand all three when you apply for the right permits. Manufactured homes were originally known as mobile homes but that changed in the 70s. This type refers to homes mounted on a chassis of a trailer. This home is built in a factory and then shipped to the location of the property on a chassis so it can be installed.

Modular homes, on the other hand, are built in a factory, but they are transported to the location for assembly on a more permanent foundation. Each type has certain codes and standards, and you need to understand which of those your shipping container home must follow so you can work on getting the necessary permits.

How to Start

Without getting into too much detail, every city in every country around the world has its own set of rules and zoning regulations, and we can't list those. In order not to overwhelm yourself, you should understand where to start and how you can work on getting the permits so you can construct your home. You should work on getting this out of the way as soon as possible. No rules will blatantly tell you not to build container homes, but certain regulations might force you to alter your design or change your mind about something concerning the home. This is why you have to get the permits first and *then* start the construction, not the other way around.

1. Learn about the relevant entities

You can't hope to get the necessary permits without knowing where to apply or who you should deal with. Each country has its own relevant entities that deal with zoning laws and grant building permits; learn about those around you to avoid costly surprises down the road. If you're trying to build a shipping container home in the US, for instance, your first destination should be the public works office. The problem with building anything in the US is that you will always need a building permit if you're within zoning codes. When you go to the public works department, they will inform you of the zone your land falls in and the necessary requirements to move forward. There is the slight possibility that your location is outside zoning codes, and it is in this rare case you won't need building permits, so you can go right ahead and build immediately. One problem with building in these locations is that they don't always have access to water or power facilities, and the internet will probably be a challenge; those are downsides you have to remember.

As for the UK, you must get permission from the local council, or else you might find yourself in a tough spot, forced to change your design or make other major changes that can cost you a lot of time, money, and effort. *Any* structure in the UK requires permission from the local council, so always remember to get one first before moving forward with your shipping container home. They will let you know of any requirements or codes you have to meet for your structure to be compliant, which will help you move forward easily.

2. Understand What Might Be Regulated

Depending on where you are in the world, there are certain parts or items in your shipping container home that might be regulated or subjected to building codes, and you have to understand those in advance so you can take the necessary steps. These following requirements might not apply where you are, but some (or all) might be.

Accessibility: Some building codes require that your shipping container home be accessible to people with disabilities; you might have to meet some requirements to make that happen before getting your permits.

Offsets: This is one you should know before getting the land (or containers if the land is already there). The distance from the property line to the edge of the house or adjacent structures might be limited by regulations, so you need to know those as well so you can design your home or choose land accordingly.

Appearance: In some areas, the color or even style and materials used to build your home might be subject to certain building codes or Homeowner Association bylaws, so you have to know the general appearance guidelines before beginning the construction process.

Dimensions: Just like with a regular building, there will most likely be certain dimensions you cannot exceed for your shipping container home. You can't just stack nine containers over one another and block the view for your neighbors. From the square footage to the maximum allowable height, there are size restrictions you must get acquainted with.

Utilities: Plumbing, electricity, and HVAC systems most likely have codes and requirements to follow, and you have to learn those before installing those systems in your container home.

Landscaping: While we all would love to plant as many trees and flowers around our homes as possible, it is not as simple as that. Landscaping has certain requirements as well that might limit your options, and it's not just about the trees you can plant, but also those you can remove for your construction to go forward.

Safety: Most building codes will have certain requirements for fire and smoke protection. You may find codes requiring some smoke detectors and a certain type, plus additional safety implementations that might be required as well depending on where you are like carbon monoxide detectors.

Structural integrity: building codes might also include compliance with certain measures to ensure protection against wind and snow loads and water resistance, and you will need to comply with those for your own safety – not just to get a building permit.

3. Documents you might need

To apply for a building permit, there are general documents that you will need, so you have to get those in order. Depending on where you are, you might need more or less than these, but in either case, you need to be prepared with whatever paperwork needed so you can get on with the construction process soon.

Site plan: So that the relevant authorities can be certain that your location meets the building standards, be sure to have the original version of the site plan, and several copies just in case.

Structural engineering plans and approval: Not everyone can draw up sound structural engineering plans, and you will need an expert to do that. Those will also be required to get your building permit so the relevant authorities can be certain that you will not build something that might be hazardous to you and everyone involved.

There are other documents you will need, like fully dimensioned working drawings that show in detail just how your shipping container home will turn out. You'll also need building regulation drawings done to scale. Expect to be asked for them before and after elevations to show how your structure will change the location. These are just general documents you should have ready no matter where you are in the world. You might be asked for more, but chances are, the above-mentioned ones will always prove useful if you have them on hand; you *will* be asked about such things.

Chapter 2: Planning

Self-Build or Contractor Build

Now that you have the necessary permits and have selected a few shipping containers, it is time to start designing your home! But before you get into that, there is a very important question that needs to be asked. Should you embark on this journey yourself with a DIY mindset, or should you get contractors to help you do the job? There isn't really a simple answer, and each approach has its pros and cons. Depending on your situation, and budget, you will need to choose to either go at it yourself or get professionals to help you do it.

1. DIY

Pros

Cheaper: the biggest advantage of a DIY approach and why many people choose this is that it is simply *much cheaper.* You don't spend money on contractors and designers to make your shipping container home, but do most of it yourself. Any money you save can buy fancier furniture and improve the design, which many prefer since the quality of the home comes first.

Confidence in the outcome: When you build the home yourself, you know how everything was done, right down to the light bulb installation! You don't have to worry about hiring contractors who might worry more about the money than doing the job right, and you can rest assured that no shortcuts were taken. It is much more reassuring in terms of the critical aspects of the construction process like roofing and insulation because you know that those were done right, so you won't have to worry about getting someone to fix any problems a few months later.

Creative freedom: Designing your own home, you have full creative control. You might think it'd be the same with contractors, but that isn't always the case. More often than not they make judgment calls and take decisions that might not particularly align with your vision for the home, but this isn't the case when you DIY. You can design the container home however you like it, no matter how quirky or absurd the design might seem—it is *your* place; do it how you like!

Cons

Significant effort: Taking a DIY approach to building a shipping container home can be taxing on so many levels. You will need to spend significant time - at first - learning about the process and the steps you need to take to do this right. Then, you will get to work, which isn't as fun or easy as it seems. Many people quit halfway through and ask the experts for help because it is just too exhausting and demanding a job, so this is something that you need to remember.

Lack of experience: Unless you're a handyman by profession, your lack of experience and knowledge will prove quite the obstacle and will make this a daunting task. Sure, there are thousands of DIY videos and articles out there, but any step you take will be breaking new ground because this is all new to you. This is why taking a DIY approach to building your shipping container home is recommended if you have any previous DIY experience, not necessarily in building container homes, but know your way around tools and be able to work with your hands.

Time-consuming: Needless to say, this is a very time-consuming task that will take up a big chunk of your time for a few months. This isn't always easy for people with full-time jobs, and it might prove too costly for someone with a job to do this in their free time. If you think you can do it while juggling a job or other responsibilities, then go for it, but just know what you're getting yourself into because this is no easy task.

2. Hiring Contractors

Pros

Experience: When you hire a contractor to oversee the work on your shipping container home, you get all their years of experience and knowledge working for your benefit. They have done this before or similar jobs at least, and they know what might go wrong and how to avoid such problems. Their expertise often proves quite valuable and can help you ensure even greater quality for your home.

Saving time and effort: Hiring a contractor saves you a lot of time and effort. They will oversee the construction process while you can tend to more pressing matters.

Functionality: The great thing about hiring contractors is you not hire them for the *entire* construction process. You can get them for just the parts you need or can't do on your own, like roofing or welding.

Cons

Expensive: Contractors don't come cheap; the cost is significant, especially when compared to the DIY approach. This may compromise your budget. If you're getting a contractor for things like electricity, plumbing, windows, doors, and painting, this might cost you anything between $50 and $150 per an hour of their time, so do the math.

Good ones are somewhat rare: While there is an abundance of contractors, finding good ones doesn't always prove easy and it can be time-consuming. It is still an important step, though, because you have to get highly qualified ones for your home.

The choice is yours. If you get a contractor, it will cost you, but you get your money's worth due to their significant experience. The question is, can you afford one, or would you like to go with the DIY approach?

The Design

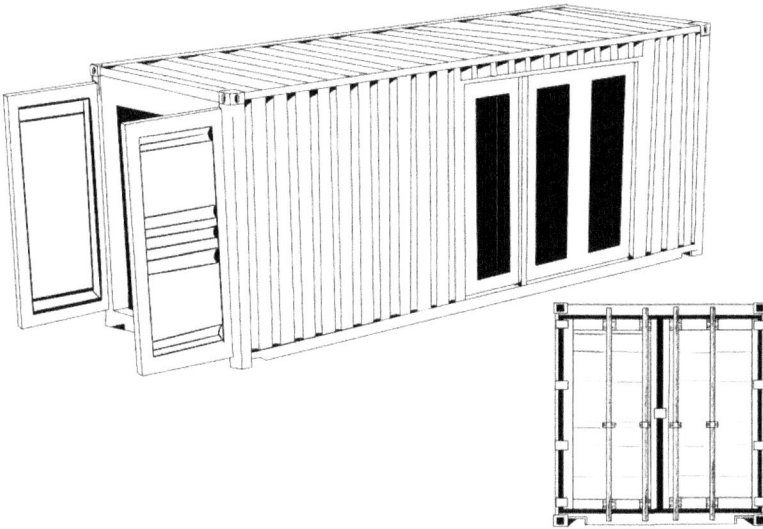

You are now ready to start the design process, which is arguably the most exciting and interesting part of this whole project. You get to try out different things and envision how you want your shipping container home to be. At this point, it is all up in the air. There are limitations to what you can do, but once you know those limitations, you can do anything within them. For instance, in the above image, the container home is made out of a single shipping container and has a special type of door with three windows. These are the kind of things you need to consider early on.

Know, though, that designing shipping container homes can be challenging. You want to make it possible to live in a small area.

This requires careful planning and understanding of architecture for you to make this work. So, where do you start?

Height

The first thing you will need to settle is how tall you want your shipping container home to be; there are countless possibilities here. Do you want a single floor home? Or do you want to go higher up to two or three floors? Most people go with single-floor container homes and stack them side-by-side rather than over the top of one another.

Width

Width is where things get really interesting. Believe it or not, it is possible for you to live in just a single container. You will need interior walls to divide the inside of the container into separate partitions, but it is possible to add a bathroom, living room, and bedroom inside the standard 20-foot container. It will be snug, but this is perfect for people who like a cozy living space.

More commonly, several containers are placed next to each other, removing the connecting walls to add more floor space and increase the size of certain rooms – or the entire house. Connecting several containers gives you more options in terms of the furniture you can get, not just the floor space. If you have a certain setting in mind that includes bigger couches or large chairs, choosing bigger floor space is recommended.

Do You Need an Architect?

The short answer is yes, but not necessarily. It all comes down to your preferences and what you want to do with the place. If you don't want to go through the trouble of designing the interior or exterior of your home on your own, then you could hire an architect. They don't cost as much as with a regular homes, considering the difference in sizes, so there's that. If, however, you want to do the design process yourself, this has its perks, too. For starters, you get to be in charge of every detail, so it will be your vision that comes to fruition. It will also prove to be less complicated than you think, so you might as well give it a go and see where your design ideas take you.

Let's dive into some example plans for shipping container homes.

These are all examples, so don't follow them if you don't want to, but they should give you ideas about how you can divide your shipping containers to make for a beautiful home.

Plans

Plan 1

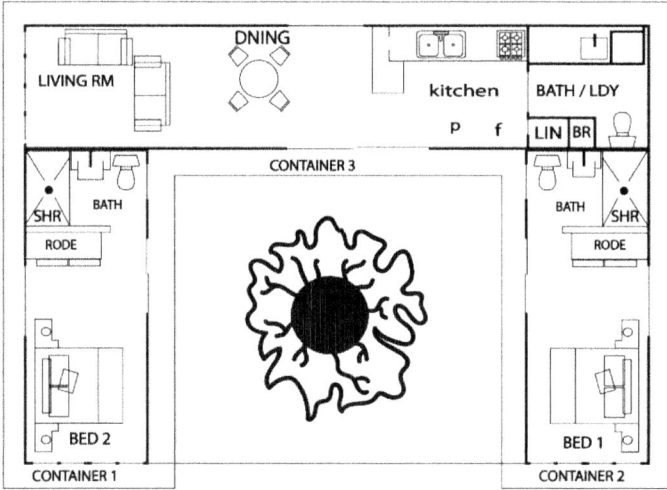

As you can see, this is a three-container architectural plan for a beautiful home with a wide area. The square footage of this home will depend on the sizes of the containers (20 ft versus 40 ft), but this one is spacious enough for a small family. That this home is made out of three shipping containers made it possible to include not one, but two living rooms and – even two bathrooms. There is also room for dedicated furniture like a dining table. The best part is you also have a wide deck area that complements the entire house.

You can bring in some outdoor furniture and make your deck area the perfect setting for a spring or fall evening. It is also ideal for barbecues and any gatherings you would like in your shipping container home.

Plan 2

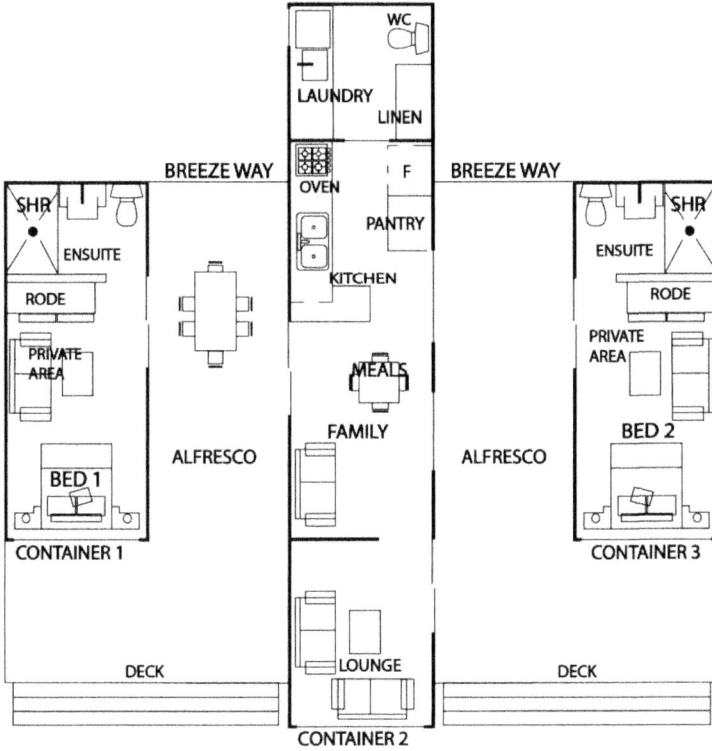

SHR ENSUITE RODE PRIVATE AREA BED 1 CONTAINER 1

BREEZE WAY

WC LAUNDRY LINEN OVEN F PANTRY KITCHEN MEALS FAMILY

ALFRESCO

BREEZE WAY

ENSUITE RODE PRIVATE AREA BED 2 CONTAINER 3

ALFRESCO SHR

DECK

LOUNGE

CONTAINER 2

DECK

This is another excellent example of a three-container home, though you might notice a difference in the size. This displays an important fact: there is no rule that says that you should buy all same-sized containers for your home. You could buy a 20 ft. one and a 40 ft. one. Or you could buy two 20 ft. containers and a third 40 ft., similar to this plan. And you can obviously get them the same sizes. The choice is yours, and you can play around with the design as you please, like in this incredible shipping container home.

This home's design puts a lot of emphasis on outdoor spaces, as evidenced in the plans. There's a lot of open space for the kids to play in or for the family to enjoy a lovely weekend together. You can spice things up a little bit and add an outdoor pool. Maybe you or your spouse like gardening, which would be perfect in a shipping container home of this design because there is room for more than one garden. As you can see, the smaller containers house the bedrooms and the bathrooms, while the middle one (the biggest) is used for the kitchen, pantry, and a lounge where you can watch TV or even have a private study or home office.

Example of open space in a shipping container home

This spacious design has considered every family member's needs, which makes it ideal for a small or medium family that wants a spacious living area without spending too much money. The catch with a design like this is that you will need to spend some time planning what you want around each section of the house. Making changes after you've started can be difficult, and it will definitely be costly. So, take your time with the design process and make sure every room is where you want it to be. Consider the space and your family's needs. For instance, a lounge might not be a good idea if you have several kids; instead, you can make this into another bedroom. Always think of your future needs, making sure the design is more functional than anything because this counts in the long run.

Plan 3

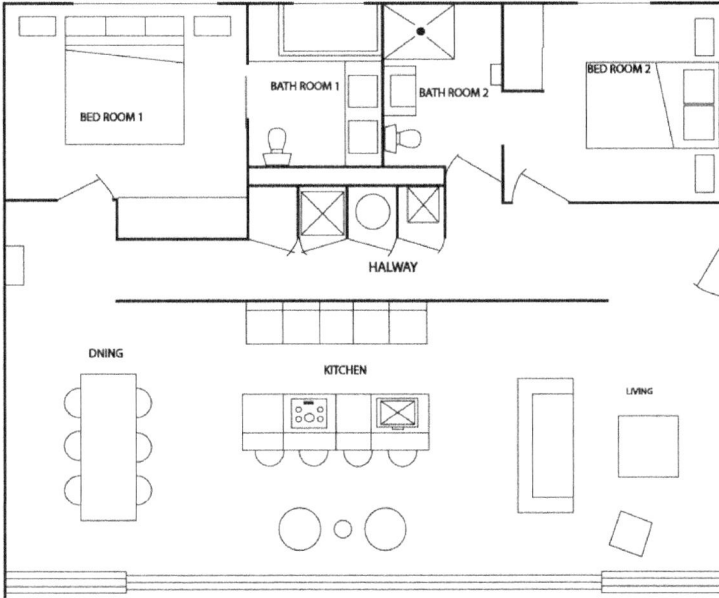

BED ROOM 1

BATH ROOM 1

BATH ROOM 2

BED ROOM 2

HALWAY

DNING

KITCHEN

LIVING

Two containers connected by a wall

This is an impressive example of a two-container home, and as you can see, the sidewall hasn't been removed from the center of the whole house. The design is simple and minimalistic, yet it makes space for several rooms and spaces around the containers that could prove functional and useful to family members. The hallway is an excellent addition that will make the place feel bigger than it is. It is also helpful that there is enough space for a dining table where the family can eat without feeling crowded—the last thing you want is for family to feel they live in a cramped space.

Plan 4

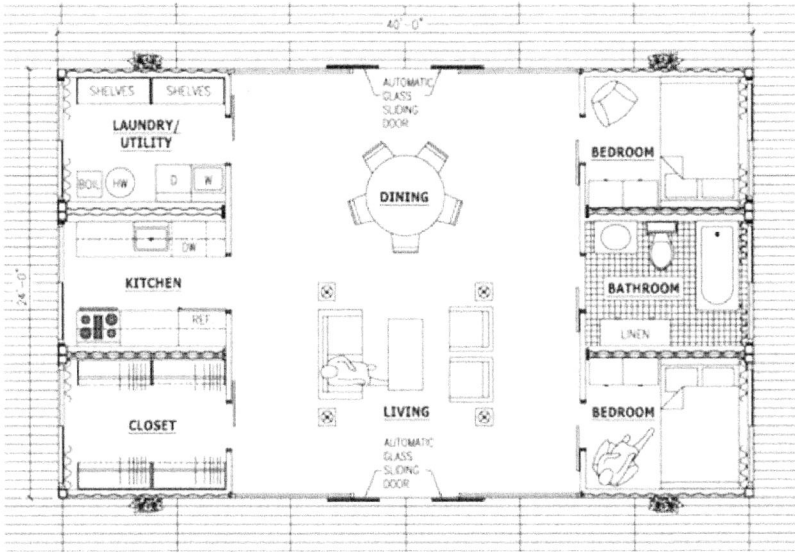

Two containers connected via a wall and with a shed roof

While this plan might look a bit fuller compared to others, it is also straightforward in nature. It utilizes two containers as well but they're put with some distance between them to make space for the living room and dining table. This open space is walled in by any type of walls you'd like to include, and the plan adds the very cool option of sliding glass doors. Those not only look elegant and are quite the addition to any container home, but they are also functional and easy to use.

Plan 5

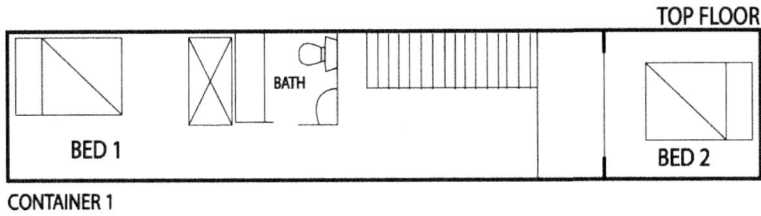

TOP FLOOR

BED 1

BATH

BED 2

CONTAINER 1

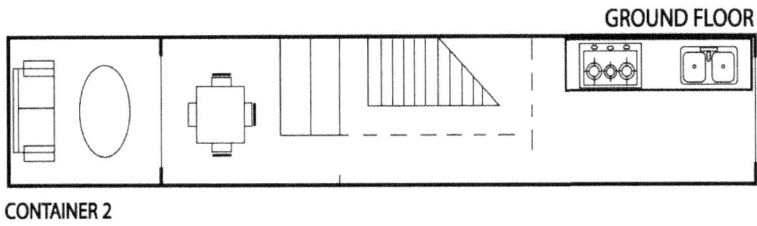

GROUND FLOOR

CONTAINER 2

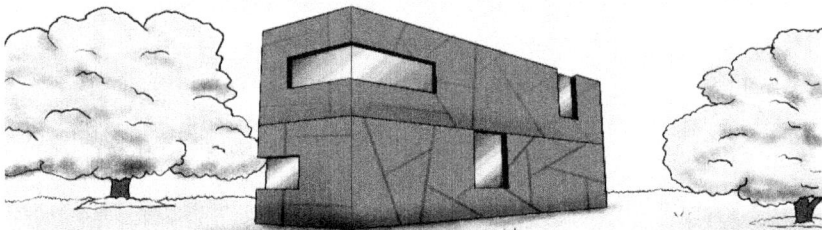

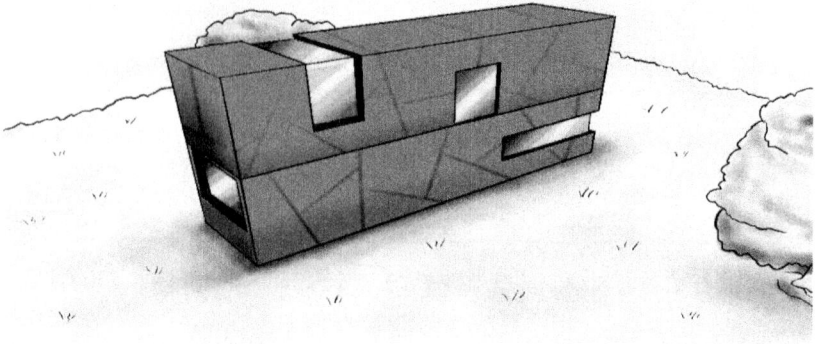

This plan shows a shipping container home with two containers placed over one the other. It looks elegant on the outside, and it's also very functional if your land space is limited and you want to make the most out of it.

Plan 6

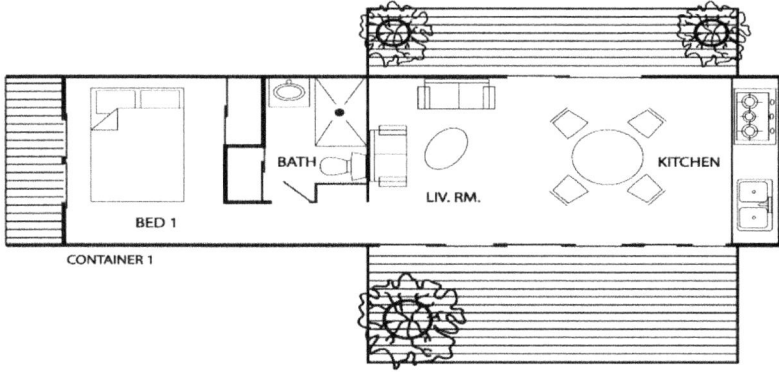

This makes the most out of space, being compact and efficient. This home consists of a single container, but the space is efficiently utilized to make room for a bedroom, living room, kitchen, and bathroom. This compact living space is ideal for a person living on their own or a couple who want to create an affordable shipping container home.

Plan 7

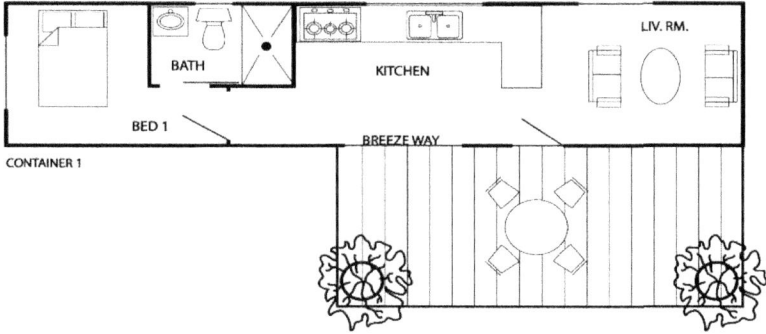

In this plan, the home is also made out of a single shipping container. However, there is room for an outer deck area, which the design utilizes cleverly. You can add a couple of chairs and a table to the deck area and use it for family meals or your morning coffee. It also gives the house quite an elegant facade, and the design is stylish and simple.

Plan 8

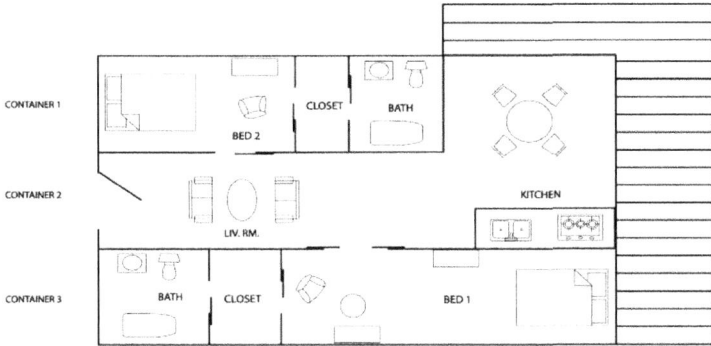

This design utilizes three shipping container to give the huge space you can see in the plan and the pictures. The first and third containers are used for the bedrooms and bathrooms, while the middle container is used for common areas like the living room, the kitchen, and the dining table. With an expanded design like this, you can have space in your shipping container home for any rooms you'd like. Though building such a home won't be cheap – it'll still be much cheaper than a traditional home.

Plan 9

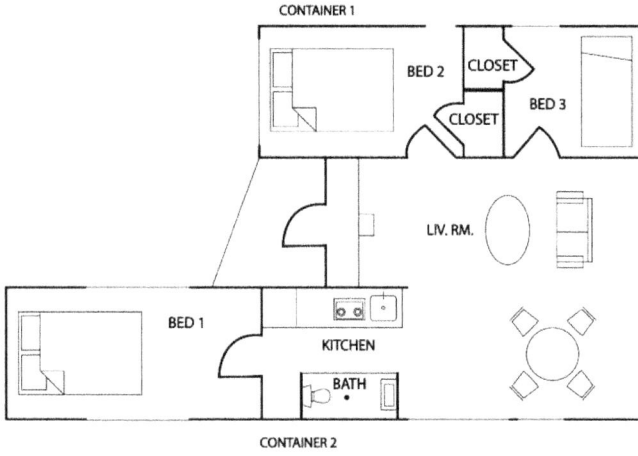

CONTAINER 1

BED 2 · CLOSET · BED 3 · CLOSET

LIV. RM.

BED 1 · KITCHEN · BATH

CONTAINER 2

Our next design uses two containers of varying size to create this elegant looking shipping container home. Despite the difference in length, there is still enough room in this home to accommodate three bedrooms, making it ideal for a family. The design also adds several floors to ceiling windows, which you can see are elegant and add to the house's overall style.

Plan 10

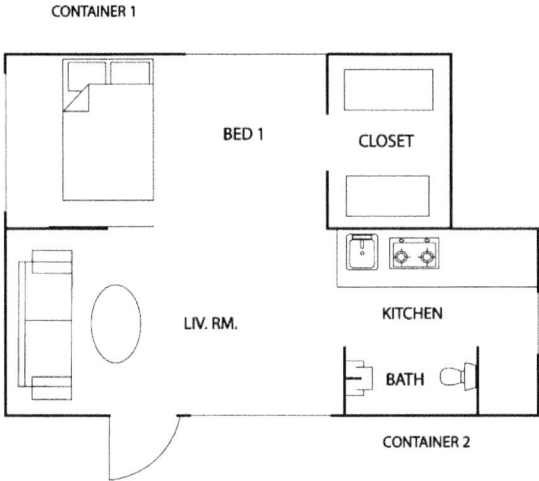

CONTAINER 1

BED 1

CLOSET

LIV. RM.

KITCHEN

BATH

CONTAINER 2

This compact design is for a shipping container home, utilizing two containers of different sizes, as is evident in the images. It has room for one bedroom and a big living room, as well as a bathroom and a kitchen. You could play around with the design if you wanted and change the rooms, but be careful because the space is somewhat limited, so you need to make the most out of it.

Plan 11

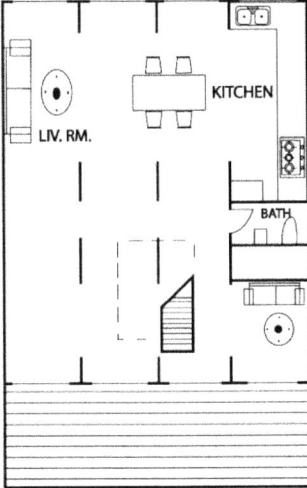

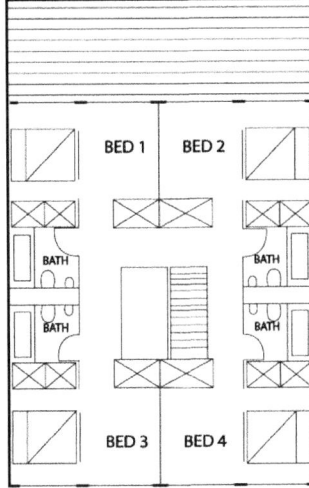

GROUND FLOOR

TOP FLOOR

Our final design is a huge shipping container home, using several containers to create a large living space. This shipping container home has two floors. The upper floor is used for the bedrooms and the bathrooms, while the ground floor is used to make room for a large living space, including another bathroom and a spacious kitchen.

This design can be much more expensive than the average shipping container home. Still, if you have the money, it is an excellent design that will make your home as big as a traditional home, while remaining less expensive.

These were just examples of plans you might consider. You could ignore them all or do one to the very last detail; it's up to you. You can also take what you like from each plan and create a design of your own with the number of containers you have in mind and that you can afford. As you can see, there aren't many limitations, and as long as you have the shipping containers, you can play around with the design and experiment however you like. You can put the rooms wherever you want, and the type of rooms you want to include depends entirely upon your preference.

Design Tips

Get full measurements: When designing anything, architecturally speaking, you need to have precise measurements. So, don't just settle for the dimensions you got from the shipping container company. Get a tape and go measure the inside dimensions yourself just in case any discrepancies might throw your calculations off. The last thing you need is for some miscalculated dimension to ruin a design you had planned out precisely. Taking precise measurements will also help you visualize the containers once they're filled with furniture and used as a home, which will help in the design process.

Prioritize: When you're starting out with your shipping container home's design, you need to make a list with all your priorities. What kind of features do you need in a home? There is a limit on the number of rooms in a single-container home, and this means you have to be specific and conscious of your priorities. Do you care more about having open spaces like deck areas or backyards, or are you more invested in the number of rooms and the available pieces of furniture? These are questions to ask before you design because every choice you make might affect the entire design.

Consider the location: having three adjacent containers looks good on paper and might give room for an impressive design, but have you stopped to ask if that is even possible on the site you've chosen? Remember to consider the location since it is the deciding factor in what you can and what you can't do with the shipping containers. You need to also measure it up precisely, so you will know what kind of area you have. It helps here if you try different combinations before starting with the design process.

Maybe you can stack the containers over one another to utilize the space you have, which might be small. There, is it even possible to stack to a certain height, or it might be illegal according to the zoning laws and permits we mentioned earlier?

Don't compromise: You need to get into the design mindset with a no-compromise attitude. You have family members, and each of them, including you, has particular needs that need to be met in your house. So, you have to do this. Maybe some like having private bathrooms or a study. Perhaps you need a home office, or your wife needs a big kitchen. Sit down with your family members, talk to them, and understand what they need so you can know how to create the perfect home that everyone will love. The more you understand the family needs, the less likely you are to compromise with those when the time to create the design is upon you.

Chapter 3: Foundations and Site Preparation

1. Soil Inspection and Preparation

If you have made it this far, you are done with most of the theoretical details in such a project. Next, it comes time to start making your home. Yet, you can't just construct the house just yet. You need to make sure the soil in the location you want to use is good and can handle the heavy loads of containers with a lot of furniture inside - plus people. It is not just the soil you have to work on, but also the foundation that will support the containers. Different foundations include rafters, piers, trench footings, and piles. Which one you will eventually use will depend on the soil in the site.

There are different types of dirt, and each requires special handling. But first things first: you need to know that the soil in your site can handle the loads over time without crumbling, which could be catastrophic. You need to have the site's soil inspected so you know if it is average sandy dirt or mixed with clay. Maybe it is gravel or even rocks. Each type of soil reacts differently to loads, determining the course of action in terms of foundation and weight distribution. Following are the most common types of soil you will encounter on various sites while building a shipping container home.

Sandy Soil

You can encounter sandy soil just about anywhere. It consisting of fine particles and there might be some rock and/or gravel in the mix. Sandy soil is considered one of the more durable types and has a high capacity to bear loads, as long as the load isn't concentrated, but instead, is spread out across a wide area. Experts recommend not digging too deep to put the foundation on this type of soil to avoid reaching softer soil if you go too deep. The best foundation to use with this soil is the rafter foundation, a very common foundation that can be easily constructed.

Clay

Unlike sandy soil, clay can be a bit more problematic because it retains water while also being fine-grained. Building on water-filled soil is risky because it is unstable and can lead to settlement in different parts of the soil. This is why dealing with clay is costly since you will need to prepare the site to handle the loads to ensure there are no future complications. Usually, you'll need to dig down to the soil that is more stable than clay, and then use pile foundations or trench footing.

Rock

Having rocky soil on site is a double-edged sword because it has its pros and cons. While rock is highly durable and has an excellent load-bearing capacity, it is also difficult to deal with. The best way to move forward is to ensure the surface is level with no inconsistencies that might hinder the foundation. Do this by stripping the surface soil and making sure the pad is leveled. The great thing about rock is it can hold heavy loads to easily support a foundation, but sometimes experts will recommend using supports nonetheless, and in that case, you should go with concrete piers. You can drill through the rock for the supports until you reach the recommended depth, and then lay your foundation.

Gravel

Gravel is the coarse material we all know, and it is excellent for drainage (one of the biggest perks here). But gravel isn't as strong as rock, so you can't build directly upon it; you will need foundation. You will dig out the gravel until you reach the recommended depth, and then you will level the surface and lay your foundation. The most commonly used type of foundation here is trench footing, which is ideal for gravel soil.

How to Determine the Type of Soil in Your Location

You can't just haphazardly determine the soil judging by its appearance, because the soil's surface may be one kind, and if you just dig a little deeper, it is something else. You must get it right from the get-go. The easiest way to do that is to enlist the help of a geotechnical engineer with the expertise and knowledge to tell you clearly and accurately what kind of soil you have on-site. They will also tell you the best foundation that goes with the soil you have, so you won't have to worry about researching yourself.

The geotechnical engineer will perform soil bores, which are done every 100 to 150 ft. depending on the engineer's take. The readings you get from those bores give you something called a soil profile to determine the kind of soil you have and, in turn, its load-bearing capacity. Soil bores often describe the soil profile up to 20 ft. This test also tells you the soil's drainage capacity (which is very important), density, current water content, the particle size of the soil, groundwater level, and the soil classification. This is basically everything that you—and more important, the expert—need to know about the soil. The information you get also includes the soil's surface qualities that will indicate the best approach to level the surface to prepare for laying the foundation.

This might sound like a lot of information to non-experts, but every detail here counts. Those numbers might be the difference between choosing the right foundation and having a safe home to getting it wrong and basically living inside an accident waiting to happen. When the soil profile is released, you will know everything you need to know from the recommended foundation depth to frost depth and other details that the average person might consider unimportant.

Understanding Foundations

You need to have a basic understanding of foundations and concrete so you can choose the right type for your soil. It is possible that the soil in your location can accommodate different foundations. So, which should you go with? The answer will depend on several factors, but you have to understand the foundations that work with shipping containers and each of their properties. *Note: this information doesn't mean you should go about this on your own. It is highly recommended that you consult with a structural engineer before doing anything with the foundations. They can help you understand the process better than anyone, and their expertise will prove invaluable here.* The foundation must be capable of carrying the structural load; understandably, you won't want to try your luck on this aspect!

1. Piers

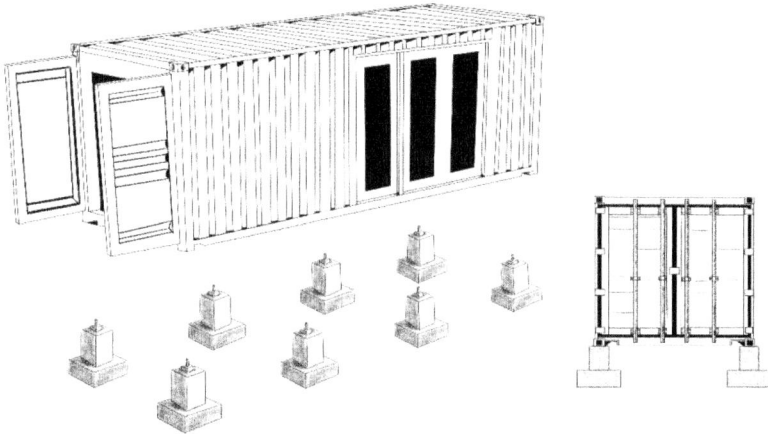

We've mentioned piers quite a few times while talking about foundations for steel containers. A pier is basically a reinforced concrete cube that you distribute at the bottom of the container in specific places to carry the loads. Traditionally, the piers are distributed at the four corners of the container and two at both sides of the center—because the middle of the container is the bearing center which has a lot of load to carry, specifically the walls. On average, for a single container, you would need six piers. The great thing about piers is that they offer a shallow foundation, which means you don't have to dig too deep (it can be costly and risky to do so).

Piers are also one of the cheapest foundation options available, mostly because you use a minimal amount of concrete for your foundation, saving a lot of money. More important, you can follow a DIY approach because they don't need a large construction crew. This is why piers are great for a soil that is a mixture of soil and gravel. Another great benefit: piers eliminate the need for insulation at the bottom of your container. This is due to the container being elevated higher than the surface level of the soil, so you don't have to worry about moisture seeping in from the underside of the container.

As we mentioned, piers are one of the most straightforward foundations and are ideal for a DIY approach. Follows is how you set up your pier foundation.

Mark the locations

This the first and most important step in setting up a pier foundation. You have to accurately mark the locations on which you will pour the concrete. Assuming you have a piece of land ready to lay the foundation, start with one stake. Drive that stake into the ground, and from it, take the measurements of your container from all four sides using string. If it is a 20 ft. container, use a 20 ft. string to move from the stake to get to the opposite pier's location. Then move from this spot with a string that is the container's width and then move the 20 ft. back again. With that, you have the four corner spots marked with stakes.

The middle two piers now must be marked. Use a tape measure to divide the string into two halves, so you'll measure 10 feet from each side. After doing this, mark the two spots on each side with stakes, and you have your center piers marked and waiting for holes.

Dig

Now that you know the locations of the six piers, time to dig. You must dig six holes around the stakes you've put. You can't have made it this far without already taking care of the soil. Whether it needs leveling or any other adjustment, this all needs to be done before laying the foundation. Assuming that's all done, dig half a meter squares around each location for the piers. Make sure that the stakes you had previously driven into the ground are at the center of each square to ensure that your placement is accurate. After that, clean the hole of any dirt, gravel, or clay.

Next, add in forms so you can pour the concrete. You can either make your own forms or purchase pre-made forms from a supplier. While forms with 0.15 cm plastic lining will be ideal, you can use wooden forms, but make sure you've built them to be solid and durable, and remember to make the holes wider to accommodate the wooden forms.

Reinforced Steel

The next part of your foundation preparation is adding reinforced steel bars, and this needs to be done slowly and accurately because these bars give the concrete its flexibility and increase its strength. There are different approaches here to placing the rebars, but a grid formation is often recommended and works best with your forms. You can add three bars across both the width and the form's length, and then you will bind the bars with a steel wire. You can use over three bars, but don't overdo it because you might make it difficult to pour the concrete if you do.

Repeat this approach every six inches by placing the rebars vertically until you have covered the whole form. Tie your grid to those vertical bars, and you will be ready for the next step.

Concrete

The next step is adding the concrete. You will fill those holes with concrete – after adding rebars to each of the six – leaving the concrete to cure for at least seven days. Curing allows the concrete to maintain an appropriate level of moisture at a reasonable temperature so the cement can hydrate. This is just the initial stage of concrete handling- wait seven days or more to add the containers.

One of the most important things you need to remember about concrete is that during the pour, it should be vibrated or rodded to avoid having air pockets that might jeopardize its structural integrity.

You will repeat these steps with every pier along the container, and after the concrete has cured, you can safely place your container. Understand, though, that you must dig the correct depth for the piers at first. Have a good understanding of the soil on the site and have dug deep enough to ensure that none of the piers will sink or crack due to soil settlement.

There is another pier: *diamond piers.*

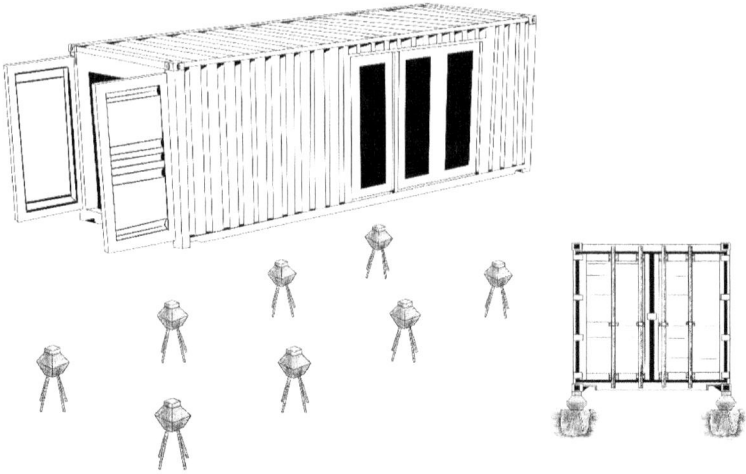

Diamond piers use a precast concrete head's strength capabilities to lock in four weight-bearing steel pins (galvanized) that transfer the load of the shipping container to a bigger area of soil compared to your traditional concrete footing.

2. Piling Foundation

There aren't any major differences between piers and piling foundation. You will follow most steps that you did with piers, with one important exception. With piles, you need to dig deeper. Some soil types can be too weak to carry loads, which is why we dig deeper until we reach stronger soil at a higher depth. In those cases, piling is a great foundation option you can use.

Another difference between piers and piles is cost. While piers are one of the easiest foundation types for a DIY approach, piling often requires costly equipment. Contrary to popular belief, you don't have to use steel piles, though they are commonly used. You can also use concrete piles, but that would require a different approach.

Concrete piles are precast at the ground level, and then you hammer them deeper into the soil. The average steel pile acts as a casing for the concrete, but it holds no load. You drive the steel tube until it is at the desired depth, and then the concrete is poured into the tube until it is filled. This is why, from afar, piles look similar to piers. This complex technique is also why piling is challenging for a DIY approach, but you won't have many options if the soil you have on-site is weak. You will need to dig deeper until you reach load-bearing depth and use piles.

3. Rafting

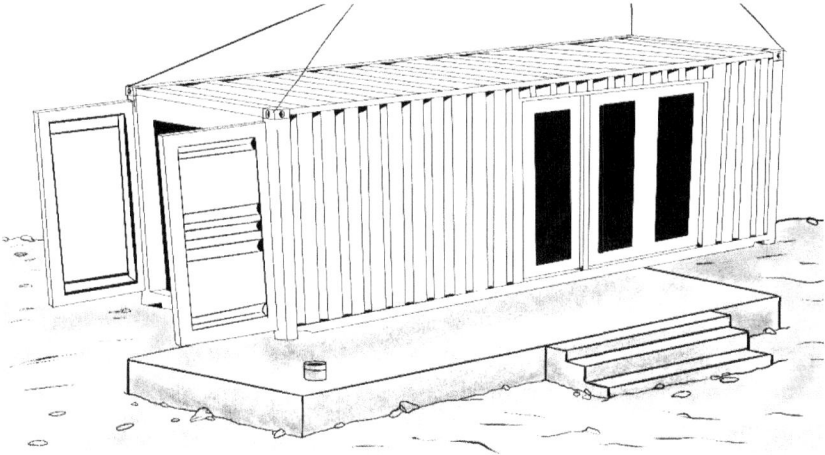

The next option is rafting, also known as slab-on-grade. It is one of the most commonly used foundation types, and it works perfectly with sandy and loose soils.

With rafting, the weight of the container is distributed evenly across the foundation. The concrete pad will support the container so you won't have to dig deeper until you reach more suitable soil, and it isolates the container from the risks of loose soil. You'll dig down to the required depth (which isn't deep with rafters), and put a layer of concrete that is the length of the container or longer, supporting the structure and carrying the loads.

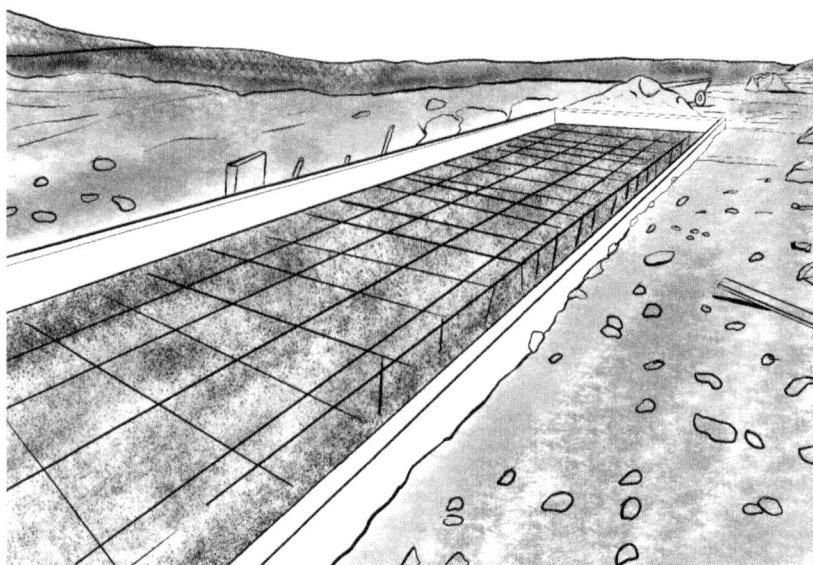

Steel grid

One con of rafters is that it is a costly approach because you will be adding more concrete than just about any other foundation type. More concrete means more steel, too, and those two aren't cheap. Unfortunately, rafters are sometimes the only option when you're dealing with loose soil, but they do their job perfectly. Rafting is also an time-consuming process. The good news is it doesn't need heavy machinery, so a DIY approach is possible here, though you will need to consult with engineers first.

4. Stem Walls

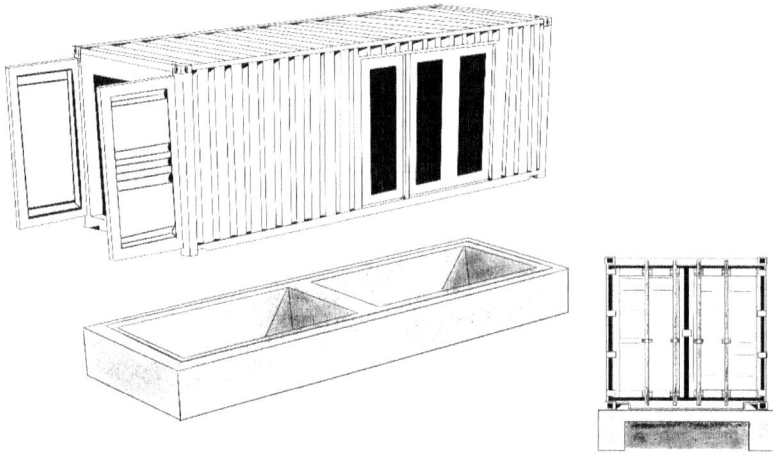

Another option for foundations, though a rarely used one, is stem walls. Stem walls are added on a concrete foundation that acts as the supporting wall that connects the foundation of a building to the vertical walls of the shipping containers lying atop. The stem wall then transmits the structure's loads to the foundation that distributes it over a larger area.

Preparing the Soil

The first thing you need to do is consult with structural and geotechnical experts that will advise you on the recommended depth for your stem walls. They will also tell you what spacing to use with the reinforced steel bars. After digging to the required depth, get to work. Level the ground and make sure it is compacted as much as possible. You need to be cautious while preparing the soil because the depth has to be precise, and you also need to make sure you have the dimensions right. Digging a too-small hole for the rafter means you will have one that might be shorter than the container which can cause problems down the line.

Add Forms and Steel

Next, add your forms to enclose the rafter-sized hole to contain the concrete you will be pouring later. Then add your steel rebars and tie them together throughout the pad. Don't "wing" this; follow accurate measurements because the steel needs to be placed properly so it can sustain the heavy load of the container.

Add Concrete

Last but not least, pour the concrete and fill the form.

Note: A very important thing you must remember is sewage and water line placement. You must run those through the rafter before pouring the concrete. This is a challenge you'll encounter with raft foundations. Both piers and piles are elevated from the soil level, so there is no worry about utility pipes. But raft foundations run through the ground under your home, and you must add those pipes before you do anything. If you don't run the sewage and water lines before you pour the concrete pad, you might well be forced to destroy it and do this all over.

Another challenge you might face with rafters is the heat. The container is placed directly on the pad, which can be create an underlying heat source in hotter months of the year. This is why you need to insulate your container's underside when using rafters properly. We will discuss insulation later in the book.

5. Trench Foundation

The last type of foundation we will be discussing is the trench foundation, also known as *spread footing*. Perhaps the trench foundation takes the best of both worlds from raft and pier/pile foundations. It is also considered extremely durable, providing a great deal of structural stability to both the foundation and the container that will sit on top.

Trench foundation distributes the load over an area much larger than piers and piles, making it safer and with more load-bearing capabilities. The great thing about this foundation is how it saves time, materials (think money), and energy, and it is done at a much faster rate than rafting. Trench foundation basically provides support for the exterior walls of the container, and because it covers a greater area, the load is distributed over more space.

If you are dealing with soil with poor drainage, you can add a layer of gravel in the bottom of the trench, which will help you drain water without jeopardizing the trench foundation's structural capabilities.

Tips on Handling Concrete

While you need not study civil engineering to create your shipping container home foundation, you need to understand concrete and its properties so you can avoid making any mistakes that would jeopardize your home's structural integrity. These are some tips that will prove useful whenever you are handling concrete.

Never forget rebars: We mentioned earlier the importance of adding reinforced steel bars to increase concrete flexural strength, but you must understand what can happen without the addition of rebar. Concrete has excellent load-bearing and compression strength, and it can withstand huge loads that many other materials cannot. Unfortunately, concrete doesn't work so well when it comes to bending. In other words, if the load is directly on the concrete, it will hold, but if the load is uneven on either side and applies bending forces, it will crack.

This is why you must always add reinforced steel bars since they have excellent flexural strength. The two materials will work together and help provide you with the load-bearing abilities you need for your shipping container home.

Perfect curing: Concrete curing is integral for it to withstand the load you will add later, and it has to be done right. While concrete gains most of its compression strength within the first day of pouring, as we mentioned earlier, you have to leave it for at least seven days until it completely cures. If you add loads before that, it will most likely crack and might even suffer failure. Another important aspect that many people forget or don't know is that curing happens at certain temperatures.

This means you can't just let the concrete cure in the sun and hope for the best. So, if you will be making concrete in hot or warm weather, you need to add some form of shading to cover the concrete so it can cure properly since heat can interfere with the curing process. You can use a blanket or a gazebo or anything that will protect the curing concrete from the scorching rays of the sun.

Mix properly: If you didn't already know, concrete is a mixture of cement, sand, and gravel. You then add water, and a chemical reaction happens between the water and the cement and the concrete begins to harden. This mixture isn't created haphazardly and there are certain ratios required so you can make strong, durable concrete. Adding in too much water to the concrete mixture will cause lower compressive strength, reduced durability, and a host of other problems. But adding in too much cement will cause thermal stresses affecting the concrete which will lead to cracking that might be severe in certain areas.

Get your ratios right. Generally, add 15-20% cement, 60-75% aggregate (sand and gravel), and 15-20% water.

Take the weather into consideration: Before you pour concrete in colder areas, you need to make sure there isn't any water or ice accumulating in the foundation hole because it might interfere with your calculations. Also, cover the concrete with blankets because you don't want it to crack from the excessive cold. However, if you're pouring in warmer areas, you need to cool the ground, if possible, before you add the concrete. You should also mix it with *cold water.* It also helps if you pour at night or early mornings in warmer climates to avoid having the sun disrupt the process.

On-site mixing versus delivery: You have two options for mixing concrete. If the quantity isn't that small, you can do it yourself. Mixing concrete manually can be done using either your hand or a cement mixer. If you are handling significant amounts of concrete, though, you should have it delivered to the site, or else you might not pull this off on your own!

Add steel plates: Another good idea involves adding steel plates at the foundation's corners before it completely hardens. This will help you weld the container to the concrete foundation, thus increasing its stability and durability.

Calculating the required amount of concrete is a bit tricky, and you should hire an expert to guide you on this step. The needed amount of concrete will vary depending on the type of foundation you're going with; it's important to make the correct amount of concrete. Too much or too little can hinder your foundation-setting process.

Chapter 4: Insulation

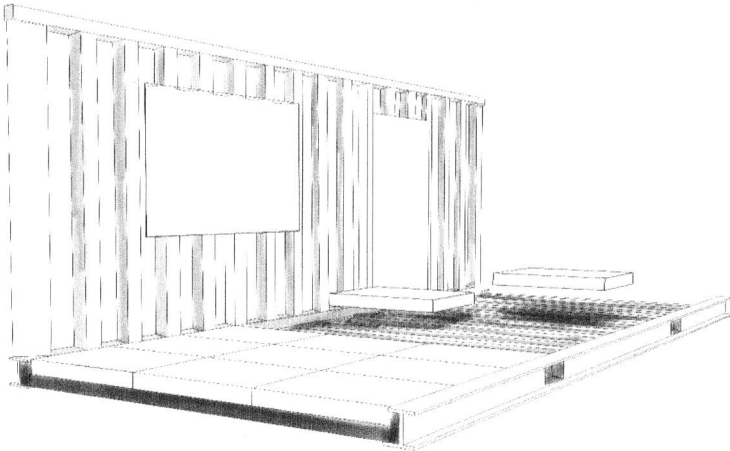

Insulating your shipping container home isn't really a luxury. Whether you live in a hot or cold area, shipping containers can easily transmit heat (or cold) and make your life miserable! There is also the problem of drainage and the possibility that water might leak into the container, whether from its roof or the underside. This is why you have to take insulation seriously and work hard to ensure that your container home is well-insulated. That way, the weather won't be a problem and won't affect your daily life, neither will underwater sources or rainwater.

There are different approaches to insulating shipping containers, and it is trickier than you might think. The main challenge faced when trying to insulate a shipping container is how thin the walls are. Yes, they are sturdy and durable, and they will carry the loads when it is time, but those container walls are also pretty thin, which makes insulation complicated. There is a way around this, but it might mean taking up some of the container's interior space.

Another factor you need to consider while looking for a suitable insulation material is how you plan on building your walls. You will go with different approaches depending on whether you will be adding several containers together; if so, the necessary room for insulation becomes less of a problem. This won't be the case if you're making a snug single or double-container home. In those cases, it is possible to add exterior insulation.

You can use different materials to insulate your shipping container home, whether on the outside or inside.

1. Cork Insulation

Cork is natural insulation that provides good results. The great thing about cork is that it is renewable and a natural source that is biodegradable since it comes from trees. More important, you don't have to cut down the trees down to get the cork. Another significant features of cork insulation is its acoustic properties, forming an acoustic buffer in your home that will stop sound from leaking outside or coming in from outside. This is particularly important for shipping container homes because those thin steel walls can easily leak sound.

2. Spray Foam

Spray foam is one of the most popular approaches to insulating containers, and it is one of the fastest ways to do it. The great thing about spray foam insulation is that it's applied to your container's interior and exterior walls. This is useful if your container has been coated with paint that can sometimes have toxic organic volatile compounds added to help the steel survive long periods in the sea. With spray foam insulation, you can contain such compounds and stop them from spreading into your home.

There are different types of spray foam insulation. It is generally a good idea to invest in a the best available because it can prolong your home's life, protecting you from several things. Icynene is generally considered one of the best options for spray foam insulation. It is a water-sprayed foam insulation that uses tiny plastic bubbles to fill the insulation's interior, providing excellent insulation and protection. It also doesn't have as many organic volatile compounds as other spray foam products, and those that are there can disappear after only a few weeks.

3. Wool Insulation

This is one of the natural approaches to insulation, and it also yields good results. Wool insulation is renewable and completely natural, seeing as it comes directly from sheep's wool. This insulation is environment-friendly and quite efficient, providing powerful insulation comparable to denim, fiberglass, and other fibrous insulation options. Another great advantage of wool insulation is that it naturally contains lanolin, which is a flame retardant. This means you don't have to treat the insulation with other chemicals for fire protection.

Carefully consider your options before you purchase wool insulation because some types are better than others. Look for companies that sell wool insulation and research the different varieties they offer before settling on a particular type.

4. Cotton Insulation

Cotton is another natural source of insulation that is environment-friendly and efficient. An advantage cotton offers is that it can be recycled from other clothing sources, so you don't need to source new cotton; pretty great for the environment! Like wool, cotton provides excellent insulation comparable to fibrous insulators like fiberglass. Like wool, boric acid (a natural fire retardant) is usually added to cotton in commercial denim, which means you don't have to treat it for fire protection. The downside to cotton is you have to make sure it doesn't get wet because moisture causes it to lose some of its insulation properties.

5. Fiberglass

Fiberglass is made from superheated sand, and, in other cases, recycled glass spun into thinner fibers. It is cheap wall insulation that is also pretty efficient, which is why it is very popular in many countries.

Cellulose

Cellulose is a loose-fill insulation that relies on adding macroscopic materials in the walls' cavity. The chunks of the insulating material are added, but for this insulation, the wall cavities need to be completely contained, or else the material will just spill on the floor. Cellulose is made of recycled paper products that get shredded and then blown into the cavity using a specialized machine.

Factors Affecting Choice of Insulation

Choosing insulation for your home is a major step in this construction process, and you need to take your time and do it right. Insulation is integral to keeping your home at a moderate temperature compared to the outdoors. Each type of insulation has its own pros and cons, and you need to consider the advantages and disadvantages before picking a certain type. These are some factors that might affect your choice.

R-Value: This industry term refers to thermal resistance per unit area. It is basically a number that expresses how well a material can prevent the transmission of heat. For instance, cotton and wool have an R-value of about 3.5 per inch, which is good. But spray foam has an average R-value of 3.7 per inch - even higher with certain varieties. As you can see, the values differ, and this is a number you need to consider while selecting insulation.

Performance: The performance of the insulation isn't just affected by its R-value. Other factors come into play, like the open or closed-cell structure of the material (for open-cell foam R-value is 3.2-3.7 per inch, while for closed-cell foam it's 6.5-7 per inch), entrapped gas, and others. These aspects affect performance characteristics, and you need to consider each before investing in a particular type of insulation.

Air leakage: Good insulation should be able to stop air from flowing through it or around its edges.

Cost: As with the rest of this shipping container home project, cost is something that you must consider. This doesn't just include the materials cost, but also labor and equipment expenses if you won't be able to do it yourself with your tools at home. For instance, spray foam insulation's average cost is around $0.5 per board foot for open-cell spray foam, and $1 to $2 for closed-cell spray foam. If you're having professionals install it for you, their time will also be factored in the expenses. Still, spray foam is considered one of the more expensive options compared to the rest. Cellulose costs $1 - $1.3, fiberglass is $0.64 - $1.2, rockwool is $0.9 - $1.65, cotton is $0.76 - $1.4, and wool is $1.33 - $2, all per square foot.

Ease of installation: How easy it to install this insulation? If it is easy, then you can DIY and save money on labor and equipment. If it is too complicated, you will need help. While the obvious choice is to save money, your shipping containers might need a special type of insulation that will require outside help. Blanket insulation is generally considered the easiest to install, and it is available in fiberglass, wool, and fibers. On the other hand, spray foam is not as easy and is not recommended for a DIY approach because it requires experience and skills, so you'll most likely have to hire someone to do it for you.

Net interior space: This refers to how much space remains in the interior of your container after applying the insulation – IF you applied it on the inside.

Vapor permeability: Can vapor flow through the insulation? How well does the insulation prevent the vapor from seeping inside and lingering there? Materials like fiberglass, wool, and cellulose are considered semi-permeable, while mineral wool is a retarder, as are most foam types, except cementitious foam, which is considered vapor-permeable.

Sustainability: We mentioned earlier that some insulation types are more eco-friendly than others, which is an important factor to consider for many people. A lot of shipping container homeowners choose sustainability for minimal impact on the environment, so the insulation's sustainability might be a factor to consider.

Types of Insulation

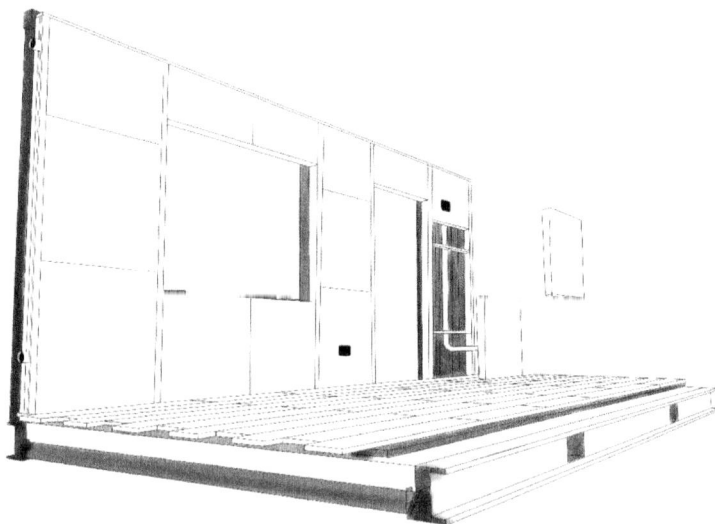

Wall and ceiling insulation application

When you think about insulating your shipping container home, you have to think about what approach you want to follow—interior, exterior, or both. Considering that shipping container homes are basically metal boxes, they are excellent conductors of heat. So, the best approach will be to insulate both the interior and the exterior of the container for the best results. This is especially important if you live in extreme weather conditions where choosing just one type of insulation would lead to heat control problems in your home.

External Insulation: The concept of external insulation is simple. If you don't have it, the container will easily heat up. Relying just on the internal insulation will lead to heat or cold seeping in through the internal insulation, affecting your entire living situation. This applies to both summer and winter, and things will be much worse if you suffer from extreme seasonal changes where you live. In short, external insulation will help keep the home cool in summer and warm in winter. This also means it will reflect on your energy expenditures; you'll save on heating/cooling costs with proper inside and outside insulation.

Another cool feature of external insulation is that it can help improve the outer facade of your shipping container home. One approach that some people follow is filling the voids of the corrugated container wall with insulation, spray foam most likely, and after that, it will be ready for paint or cladding. This is, however, a somewhat more expensive option that might not work with all budgets.

It is also important to insulate the container's underside because a lot of heat and moisture might seep in or out from there. The best time to do that is when placing your container on the foundation. If that doesn't work, you have another option of adding insulation underneath the flooring, which we will discuss later. In any case, make sure there is some form of insulation on the underside of the container.

While we recommend insulating both the interior and the container's exterior, some people prefer saving inside space by only doing exterior insulation. Not modifying the container's internal walls does preserve a lot of floor space, but, you need to make sure your external insulation is done properly. External insulation will help you preserve that floor space while providing some heat control. Remember that you will also need to insulate your container's roof, whether you are leaving the original roof or adding a new one.

If you are adding a new roof, adding spray foam or other insulating materials underneath it should be fairly easy. If you are leaving the roof as it is, you need to cover it in an insulation layer. This is particularly important if you don't plan on adding a ceiling inside the container, since this means you won't be adding the interior insulation that comes with the ceiling—this one doesn't take up any extra height. In other words, if you don't plan on adding a ceiling, make sure the roof is well insulated.

Internal Insulation: Many people ignore internal insulation, thinking it is not really essential, but it can make a world of difference. While external insulation does the biggest job in controlling the heat or cold seeping into the shipping container, climate may still make it past that first layer; this is where internal insulation comes in. To partition and frame your container's interior, then adding insulation won't take up much space, and the same goes for when you add a new ceiling. Suppose you leave an exposed ceiling (the container's original). There, you should expect rust after a while since there will be a lot of condensation inside the container and affect the original steel ceiling.

The great thing about spray foam insulation inside your house is it can help you improve the place's aesthetic value. It can cover up any dents or scratches or any other marks on the walls, and it is easy to paint over spray foam insulation. You can use external insulation or internal in certain places or you can double up in areas such as the roof/ceiling to minimize any heat seeping into your home.

Types of insulation

We discussed earlier the different materials you can use for insulation, and now, we will list the different ways you can *use* these materials. Each type of insulation has its pros and cons. You be the judge of which works best for your home.

Blanket/Roll Insulation: this is considered the cheapest available insulation. The most commonly used material with blanket insulation is mineral, which is also known as rock wool. Installing blanket insulation inside your shipping container home requires stud walls (which we will explain in a latter part of the book). You should know that the rock wool rolls are put between the battens and then you roll them down in place. As long as you have the stud walls in place, adding in blanket insulation should be simple and straightforward.

Know, though, that blanket insulation is made out of fiberglass, so you need to treat it with caution to avoid damaging it. Always use protective gear, including masks, goggles, and gloves. Compared to insulation types like spray foam, blanket or roll insulation is considered somewhat cleaner, but it is more time-consuming than spray foam and a bit more complex.

As we just mentioned, to install blanket insulation, you need to have stud walls in place. After that, you will simply place the blankets or rolls in the gaps between the studs. The great thing about this approach is that you can insulate the wall without cutting anything, which reduces the time needed for this process and is generally less wasteful. Still, plan ahead and calculate the battens and blankets' width so you can do this with no cutting. Since you are using blanket insulation, it is always recommended to put the foil against the container's wall.

While it is recommended to use spray foam insulation at the underside and top of the container, you can use blanket or roll insulation – but you will need to add battens first. So, add the beams across the width, whether that is on the top or bottom of the container and space them at a distance of 1.5 inches between centers. Some people mix between different methods, using spray foam and blanket insulation together. You just put the panel or blanket on the foundation or roof and add a thin layer of spray foam.

Spray Foam: We talked earlier about spray foam and how it is one of the best insulation approaches - and the fastest. However, spray foam insulation is also a bit tricky and requires some skill and experience so you can install it properly. It is also somewhat messy and can cover places you don't want covered with foam. This is why it is recommended that you always cover such areas while working with spray foam. Be careful to cover pipes, wires, windows, doors, electric sockets, and any other area or item in the shipping container you don't want covered in spray foam. Using a plastic sheet, cut-to-size, is an effective way of protecting those areas. Also, remember also to cover the floors with plastic before you add the interior insulation so don't clean up any mess later on. Pro tip: cover cables and sockets and pipes with tape before spray foaming.

One great thing about spray foam insulation is it not needing battens, which means you can spray it directly on the walls and save a lot of time otherwise spent making the battens. It is also an excellent insulator that does a better job that most insulators out there. This is because spray foam provides an airtight barrier and the best heat resistance per thickness among other insulators. Another great advantage of spray foam over blankets is how easily you can use it to fill gaps and even out uneven surfaces, unlike panels or blankets which need to be cut to fit into such confined spaces.

You don't have to frame the inner sides of external walls to insulate with spray foam; if you do, it will allow you to install plasterboard or paneling over the insulation. Plasterboard will offer an even and smooth surface you can paint, and panels also have their own special look that can be left as is. If you follow this approach, spray foam into the space between the battens like you would were you using blanket insulation.

Using spray foam insulation, you should add at least a two-inch layer of foam thickness on the wall. You can spray foam the full two inches on one side of the wall, or you can divide it between the interior and exterior walls by adding one inch on the inside and the second on the outside. Remember that spray foam can seal any gaps that result when you join two containers —around bolts and joints, and adjoining floors.

Panel Insulation: This is your third option. It is a bit more expensive than blanket insulation, but cheaper than spray foam. It is also one of the rather less complicated means of insulating walls in your shipping container. One advantage is that it is quickly set up, and it is not as fragile as fiberglass. Panels are somewhat thin, but they do provide very good insulation. You can get them in fixed sizes and place them between the studs as you did with blanket insulation, and the installation process is pretty much the same. Consider the fact that panels are thinner, so you will have more space to work with, unlike blanket insulation. You can use panels to insulate the container's underside, too, just like blanket insulation, but you need to add battens to the foundation to affix the panels.

Other Approaches to Control Heat

You will notice we have discussed insulation and controlling the shipping container's heat even before talking about handling the container when delivered. This is because insulation or maintaining a container's temperature are critical aspects you need to keep in the back of your mind even before receiving the containers. However, there are other approaches to tackle the temperature situation inside your containers that don't include insulation.

Plants

While you must plant trees, flowers, and plants around your home, that doesn't mean you can't do the same inside or on your shipping container home. One of the best ways to control the heat inside shipping containers is to invest in greenery. You can create a green roof -a garden on the roof of your home with plants and grass. While the greenery won't work as an insulator, it can reduce the thermal radiation coming in from the sun into your house. You can also do this even if you have insulation because a green roof is an excellent idea whether it is aesthetically speaking or to supplement your insulation with fresh air and reduced heat.

You can implement other techniques in the design of your house, like passive heating and cooling design. In this approach, you design your container home so it dampens the energy needed to heat or cool the place. This can be done using techniques like solar chimneys and Trombe walls, among others. This approach is great in moderate climates, but if you live in an area where there is constantly high temperature and scorching sun, it won't be sufficient on its own.

At the end of the day, insulation is your best answer for controlling heat in your shipping container home. There are a ton of options, and even the limited types of insulation we mentioned have subcategories and derivative compounds. While insulation is critical to your home's design, you shouldn't dwell on it for too long because there are other pressing matters to attend to. The important thing is to make sure that insulation works within the grand scheme of your design, choosing a type that will work for your particular home.

Chapter 5: Receiving the Containers

If you've made it this far, then you are good to go in terms of receiving the containers and prepping them to execute your design. By now, you know what kind of foundation you need and how you will be insulating your containers. Most important, you have a certain design in mind, and all that is left is for you to get the shipping containers you have selected, and you can get to work. Before we get to that, you need to understand your options for working on the container on site. Do you want to receive the container as it is, working on it yourself to cut through the walls, and install the windows and such? Or would you prefer a prefab container? Another option is working on it off-site, which means you will have a factory work on your specs and then it will be delivered to you ready to go.

1. Prefab Containers

This is the most expensive option of the three you have. You need not work on cutting the walls to make more space or install the windows yourself with prefab containers. Everything that needs to happen to the container will take place in the workshop before it is delivered to you. The great thing about this option is that it saves a lot of time and effort, and the containers delivered to you will be ready to be directly placed on the foundation you had set earlier. It also might save you money in the long run, because if you DIY, you might permanently damage the container and cost yourself extra repair money, or worse, be forced to replace it altogether.

On the other hand, if the containers are prefabricated, they are converted to the shape and condition you need with no effort. A cool feature you get with prefab services is that they often have deals with installation services, so you won't have to worry about installing a heavy container yourself or moving it from the workshop to your site. With prefab containers, you will get someone to install the container and connect them however you like, plus secure their placement so they don't fall off. Yes, this is expensive, but it is still cheaper compared to a traditional home.

2. On-Site Conversion

With on-site conversions, you will be doing most of the work yourself to create the home's shell that will be your living space. This includes everything from cutting walls to making arches and windows through the steel. You will obviously need a lot of equipment like blowtorches, sturdy drills, grinders, and a lot more. With this DIY approach, you will be saving yourself a lot of money since there aren't any additional shipping costs (if you shipped to a workshop) and you won't have to pay for labor or the machinery they use.

Another great advantage of on-site conversion is that you work on your own schedule; you can work at night, early mornings, or on weekends. You aren't bound by any workers' schedules with on-site conversion, which can prove quite useful and easy. On-site conversion is safer since you will do all the work on the container and it will already be on site. Changing the container structure often weakens its structural integrity a little, which isn't problematic if it is already at its resting place. But if you are moving it, this might lead to problems. With on-site conversion, you won't have to worry about shipping it to your location and you can avoid any accidents that might happen to the container along the road.

The biggest challenge with on-site conversion, though, is that it is difficult. You need to have a certain skill set and the necessary tools to take on such a task. If you don't have the equipment needed, you must buy it, making this more costly than other conversion options. There's also the problem with having access to power and supply in a site that might not have any yet since you might not yet have any utilities. This means you will need a generator –another significant expense if you don't already have one.

Naturally, there's the predicament of noise and the neighbors' disturbance if you are in a busy neighborhood.

While you can hire contractors to convert the containers on-site, this will be a more expensive option compared to a DIY approach. At least this way, you won't have to worry about not having the right tools for the job or the required set of skills to do it right. This is also a better option if you can't find a local workshop to do the work on your container.

3. Offsite Conversion

The last option you have to convert containers is off-site conversion. While this option is also great if you don't have the necessary tools or experience/skills to take on this task, it has its downsides as well. However, offsite conversion is great if you don't want to bother with working on making the adjustments yourself. The good news is you will have experienced professionals doing all the work, so you won't have to worry about the experience factor here. Offsite conversion can be done by you as well. You can have the container delivered to a local workshop or fabricator and work there. They'd have the necessary tools to help you, and you will also get help if you run into any roadblocks.

Another perk of offsite conversion is that your container will be kept safe. The last thing you need is for your container to get soaking wet or suffer from any other unexpected weather conditions like snow while it's being modified, which could easily happen with on-site conversion. If your container is delivered to a workshop it will be stored under a roof or indoors if there are any weather complications, so it will be protected. Dealing with a workshop—whether you will do the work yourself or have someone there do it for you—is also useful because there will be electricity on site, so there won't be a reason for you to worry about electricity and getting a generator.

On the other hand, there is always the concern that something might happen to the container after the modifications and during transport to the site. Remember: the container is more fragile after conversion. The workshop location might present difficulties as well; it may be far away, creating a long commute for you, regardless of whether you want to do the work yourself every day or just oversee it. Also, consider that you won't be working at your own schedule; the workshop has working hours that might not suit you or might present a problem, but you must abide by those hours (ask about working hours before you sign off with any workshop).

Shipping

With your modifications in mind and the site prepared, all that remains is delivering the container so you can get to work. While that sounds easy, it might present a few complications. For starters, where are you going to get your container from? How much does it cost?

Buy local: Many shipping container buyers mistakenly look at the container's price without taking shipping into consideration. You might find an excellent deal on a few containers in Australia, but the shipping cost would triple the money you will pay. This is why it is always best to look for local dealers because even if the prices are somewhat high, usually it will still be cheaper than buying a container in another country and shipping it to your location. Plus, shipping containers from other countries are risky and might get damaged on the way and arrive in different shape than what you've seen online.

Buying local also makes it easier since the dealer can help ensure that you get all your containers from the same company and of similar quality. Generally, it is a good idea to look around and examine several options. Don't settle for the first few containers you come across - there might be better deals just around the corner.

Cost: This will vary depending on the size of the container you're buying and where you are buying it from. These next rates are assuming you are shipping a container inside the US; international shipping rates are significantly different and need to be calculated separately.

Usually, shipping rates are fixed and are calculated for a standard distance of 50 miles. For a 20 ft. container, the shipping rates would be around $200-$250 for transporting and offloading. Distances farther than 50 miles will entail a fee per mile, around $2/mile for the total distance. If the container is 40 feet, prices are almost double that. So, it's $400-$500 for 50 miles. Prices may vary depending on the shipping company and its rates and policies. You can find a shipping company offering a flat rate for a total distance greater than 50 miles for 20 or 40 ft. container, so, shop around.

Plan ahead: Plan ahead for container shipping and delivery. You need to be around for when the container arrives so you can receive them and place them, and you don't want the shipping company to deliver them in your absence. You need to get the details of the delivery right. Some people order the container before they prepare the site in an attempt to save time. You might get the containers earlier than expected, and the soil is not ready yet. What would you do then?

Don't take any chances with container delivery. Make sure the site is ready and the conversion plan is set, and order your container at a time you are certain you can receive them, and the site will be ready. Details make a lot of difference here. If you plan on insulating the bottom of your container, the insulating material needs to be ready so you can get to work right away. Pay attention to those small details because they distinguish between a successful delivery and a lot of complications you don't need.

Container placement

You will need to place the container on your selected foundation so you can work on the shell of your home. Once the container reaches the site, you will have a couple of different approaches to place it, but you need to do it slowly and carefully.

Tilting: the first approach to properly placing the container is to tilt it into place. To do that, you will need to have it moved on a flatbed trailer, which is an option that won't cost you a lot of money. Then, assuming it is possible to do this on the site, you will ask the driver to tilt the trailer's bed so the container can slide smoothly on the foundation. This is probably the easiest, and cheapest, way to place your container on the foundation, avoiding the need for costly cranes. Consider this method when you're preparing the site and the foundations since planning increases this approach's likelihood of working. In other words, place the foundation to give the trailer space to maneuver into the site and tilt the container.

Cranes: Your second option is using a crane. This is ideal for sites without any wiggle room for the truck driver to tilt the container, and also this is how to go if you plan on stacking a couple of containers over one another because tilting won't be much good then. While cranes are a more expensive option that entails renting the machine, paying for its operational cost and the labor operating it, they are very efficient and do the job quickly and with no complications. Remember to take the size/weight of your container into consideration because there are different types of cranes and some might not be able to lift 40 ft. containers. Ask first, ensuring that you get the right piece of equipment for the job.

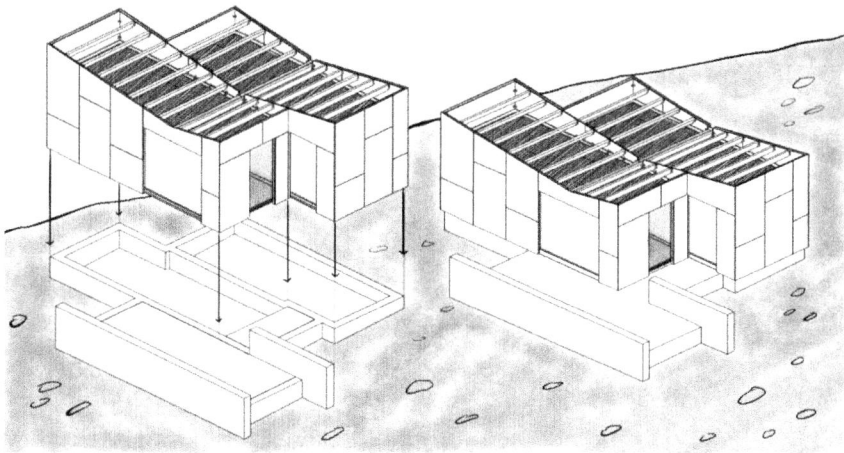

Assembly of ready-made containers on concrete base

Note

The foundation surface needs to be completely level before you can place the container. If you place the container on an uneven foundation, you must use shims and spaces to bring the container level; this complicates things. So, as much as you can, level the foundation's surface before you place the container on it.

Also, remember to add insulation to the underside of the container between it and the foundation. We talked earlier about the different options you get with insulation, and this is when you first need to apply that knowledge. Insulating the container's underside helps you control the temperature, which comes not just from the walls. After insulating the bottom, you can work your way to the interior of the container. Also, if you are placing more than one container next to each other, it is always good to add insulation between the walls of each to control the temperature and keep moisture out.

Anchoring the Containers

For safety reasons, a shipping container needs to be anchored so you can be 100% certain that it is at no risk of overturning or tilting due to unexpected weather conditions. Studies show that anchoring the container can help it withstand winds up to 150 miles per hour. Anchoring also helps minimize the chances of any damage happening due to settlement. There are different ways to anchor your shipping container, and it will depend on several factors, starting with the type of foundation you have.

Welding: this is one of the best ways to anchor shipping container and it always yields great results and provides excellent stability. We mentioned earlier the importance of adding steel plates when you pour the concrete of your foundation, and this is where those plates come in handy. After your foundation, say piers, cures and the concrete hardens, you can weld the container to the steel plate. This helps create a resilient foundation that can withstand just about anything, and it significantly increases the overall durability of your shipping container home.

Containers will need to be welded together for further stability and strength if you plan on stacking them. Generally, it is optimal to weld the container at the adjoining parts of the roof, floors, and walls. Use flat steel at those points and stitch weld, leaving no . spaces between containers. Any areas where overlapping occurs need to be properly welded so you can ensure the overall stability of the containers and that they won't sway or move against wind loads or other weather conditions.

One thing you need to know about welding is that it cannot be easily undone or altered. Once you weld those containers together, and to the foundation, there is no changing that without great cost in terms of time, equipment, and manpower. Unlike some of the next approaches we will discuss, welding is here to stay. So, remember that if you have any plans to move the container home or do changes to the overall structure; it will be nearly impossible if you've welded walls or floors to your foundation. This is the main challenge with this type of anchoring, though it provides the strongest and most stable connection between the containers or the foundation.

Bolting: It is possible to drill holes in the container's floors to bolt them to the foundation lying underneath it. The drilling is usually done around the four corners and then you can add 12-inch by 1-inch bolts. After that, you need to hammer those bolts into whichever foundation you have used, whether piers, piles, rafter, or trench. Finally, tighten the head of the bolt to ensure it won't shake loose.

As for connecting containers, you can also use bolting. It is not the cheapest option, but it guarantees stability and strength. You must bolt the containers together at adjacent corners for this to work. Drill through any corners in common between the containers, but add in a metal plate while you're drilling so it can act as a washer for the threaded sides of the bolts you will add later. Then, put in the bolts and add an additional washer on the bolt's threaded end and a nut to keep it from moving. Tighten the bolts and seal any gaps around both ends of the bolt using a sealant material.

Clamping: This is the cheapest option, but it is also the least durable and safe. Besides the fact that it is cheap, the plus side to clamping is that you can disassemble your containers and move them easily with this approach. It is not a permanent solution like welding, and it won't be as difficult to disassemble as bolting. In short, clamping is a great option if you plan on moving your container home in the future because you can easily disconnect the ties between the containers and move them to a different location.

Cleaning the Container

By now, you have your containers in place, anchored to the foundation and joined. A lot of work still needs to be done, but a good start will be cleaning the inside of the containers. As we mentioned earlier, shipping containers might transport shipments with toxic substances, and it is always a good idea to clean them before you do anything. Here's how you can do that.

Quick Inspection

The first thing you need to do is quickly go through the container's inside now that it is delivered, so you can form an idea of what exactly it needs. Take a strong flashlight, step inside, and start looking. This initial inspection will reveal more than you know. You might come across dust and pollutants, stains, seeds, pollen, or any other number of surprises. Look at the corners and inspect the walls. Don't leave anything to chance and make sure you have covered all possible angles so you could move on to the next step.

Start with the Dust

After the inspection, the first thing you will be getting rid of is the dust. There is nothing quite like those minute particles to make the air thick inside the container and cover everything in a dusty layer. So, sweep and clean any debris, dust, cobwebs, or anything that shouldn't be found inside your containers. Get the corners and dust off the roof and walls; leave no area upswept. Pro tip: wear a dust mask and goggles so you can stay safe and avoid any respiratory or eye problems while cleaning. Work your way from the back of the container to the front where the door is, and get everything out.

Use a Leaf Blower

While your initial sweep might get rid of dust and pollutants, a leaf blower or air compressor is useful for an extensive cleaning. It will use compressed air to eviscerate anything that might be stuck, like pollen, seeds, or other materials. The blower will remove detached materials that might be otherwise difficult to remove with just a broom, no matter how strong it is. After using the air compressor or leaf blower, sweep one more time so anything that fell on the floor can be removed.

Wash It Down

Dust and pollutants aside, it is more than likely that you will find stains or sticky substances that won't be removed with an air compressor. This is where you will need a pressure washer. If you don't have one, it is an excellent investment because it always proves useful. Like with dusting, start at the back of the container and work your way to the front. Get all the walls, floors, and roof and remove any stains since those might be chemical substances. Pay special attention to the corners since they collect dust, so you have to rinse them thoroughly. The floors also require your attention because there might be rust that needs scrubbing off, as well as trapped dirt.

The pressure water will also prove invaluable while cleaning the container's exterior, which will have dirt, sticky substances, chemicals, and rust. Pro tip: while using pressure washers, always wear safety goggles. Anything can bounce off the walls and into your eyes, so you must protect yourself as much as possible to avoid any accidents happening, especially considering that you're working in a closed space if you're cleaning the container's inside.

One more pro tip: Vinegar does wonders with challenging stains. If you run across one while cleaning the container, whether it is on the outside or inside, fill a bottle with vinegar solution and apply it to the stubborn stain. Leave it for a few minutes and scrub those stains away.

Fix Surface Damage

While cleaning the containers, it is possible that you might run into surface problems like small holes and dents or rust and corrosion. It is always wise to take care of those problems soon before moving forward. Check the interior and exterior for any such complications. If you ignore those problems, they will most likely grow and cause further complications down the line! You can fix small holes using a wire brush, and it is quite an easy task to do and should prove simple enough. Just remember to paint the area you used a wire brush on. As for larger holes, you can add a piece of steel to cover it – either weld it to the container or use a sealant to glue the steel to the hollow part.

For simple rust, you can fix it with rust remover and white vinegar. Just apply the vinegar or the rust remover on the infected areas and scrub away, and usually the exterior rust will be removed. You can use an aluminum foil to scrub the rust if white vinegar and a piece of cloth won't work.

Use Sandpaper

Using sandpaper isn't just to improve the container's aesthetic value, but also to avoid having complications like peeling and wear and tear exacerbate and cause more damage. Use a belt sander to tackle any parts along the shipping containers that have signs of wear or flaking and peeling. This will help you create a smooth surface much better for protecting the container against weather conditions and moisture. After using sandpaper, apply a primer coat of paint to make it stronger. A primer coat of paint protects the container against peeling, corrosion, and moisture, and it generally makes it a stronger container.

Then, after the primer coat of paint has dried, you can add exterior paint on the container's inside and exterior. Pro top: invest in high-quality paint because it will last longer and, more important, it will look good and protect your shipping container home.

As you can see, cleaning shipping containers isn't just to make them look nice, but it also improves their structural integrity and provides protection against moisture and other problems. This isn't a step you can skip, and you definitely can't just hose the container down and claim you have cleaned it! You need to be thorough while cleaning the shipping container since chemicals may have been transported, having a bad effect on your family's health. In short, clean the shipping containers properly before moving on to the next step.

Chapter 6: Services: Electricity, Plumbing, and Phone Lines

Conducting Electricity

With the shell of the containers in place, and each of them (or just the one) cleaned and ready to go, there are different ways to move forward with the construction process. One way is to work on the wiring. This is one step that needs to be done by an expert because a mistake here could prove fatal, not just costly. You need an electrician to handle the wiring and conduction of electricity for you or else you might hurt yourself doing it.

Understand Local Regulations

We talked earlier about zoning laws and regulations, and they don't just apply to constructing your home, but also to the power. You have to consider several points and a lot of requirements regarding electricity in your shipping container home (or any home). The laws and regulations about electrical conduction vary depending on the city, state, and country, so a good idea would be to inquire first thing about those laws. Go to your local planning office and ask about the requirements and what you can and can't do so you can move forward in accordance with regulations.

Electrical Plan

The electrical plan is just as important as the architectural plan, and you need to make one before you do anything electricity-related. The electrical plan is to show you where the outlets, light switches, and fuse box will be, and this is something that you have to know before running any wire through the house. The layout of that plan will depend on the home's design because each room in the shipping container home will have different uses and thus requirements. For instance, in a bathroom, outlets need to be farther from the bathtub and closer to where you will be using electrical grooming appliances and hair dryers. Lights switches around the house need to be added in comfortable locations where it is easy to reach them; adding those in the wrong place makes it inconvenient to reach.

Power Outlet

The electrical plan is crucial, and it is not something that you should ignore until it is time to work on the electricity. It needs to be done right after – or simultaneously with – the architectural plan so you can adjust either, if need be. You could be forced to swap rooms of rooms depending on electrical wiring or changing the number of switches, for instance. You need to envision how the electrical plan will look in your shipping container home before you do anything else. Understand that it is a smaller space compared to a regular home, and you need to accommodate a lot of things. So, in the kitchen, for instance, you need to make room for a light switch and specify the location of plugs for the microwave, toaster, refrigerator, stove, and oven.

Your local zoning office will require the house's electrical plan and it will be reviewed so they can make sure the electrical plan is within the codes and regulation. This is done before you can get your permits to move forward. Note: you might have to provide stamped plans from an electrician or an electrical engineer—so, even if you plan on following a DIY approach with wiring, you at least need the help of an electrician at this stage.

What Do You need?

If you will be installing the electricity in your shipping container home, there are things that you need to know. Several components will be integral, and you have to get those early on so you can start on the right foot. So, you will need electrical boxes for any outlets, fixtures, light switches, and a fuse box. While designing the plan, consider local codes on the minimum allowed distance between outlets (for safety reasons) because you might be forced to order fewer than you had in mind. There's no sense in ordering outlets you won't be using.

On average, a shipping container home could run on 100, 150, or 200 amps depending on the home's size and personal preference, but this is one thing you need to cover with the electrician. You should use just the right amount of power for your home, not more or less, to avoid safety concerns and to keep all appliances running smoothly.

Type of Wiring

The kind of wiring you will use in your shipping container home needs to be a bit different from that used in a traditional house due to the metallic nature of containers. You should also know that safety standards and requirements for electrical wiring set forth by the local authorities are stricter because you're basically living in a metal box so extra caution is required when dealing with electricity for them.

To explain further, in traditional homes, the most commonly used wiring is non-metallic sheathed cables, and those are used for outlets and circuits throughout the house. Those cables are run between the house walls and the wooden studs using boreholes, which is done safely since wood and drywall are good insulators that won't conduct electricity. Even over time, after some wear and tear, if the insulation gets damaged behind a wall, the electricity will still run normally, and safety won't be compromised.

But in container homes, the same risks exist, but there is a significant difference. Unlike wooden homes, a shipping container is made out of steel. On the one hand, that makes them less prone to bursting into flames, but this significantly increases the risk of electrocution if any bare electrical wire comes in contact with the wall which could expose the entire house and its residents to high voltage and electroshock. This is why you need to follow the guidelines in your country including all relevant local entities. It is also a good incentive to consider hiring an experienced electrician to work on your wiring and electrical system because their expertise will prove valuable.

If you have experience in dealing with electricity and would like a DIY approach to installing your container home's electrical system, we will explore your options. In generally, your container home will be connected to either a local grid or an off-grid system like solar panels, and each has its own regulations and approaches.

Connected to a Local Grid

If your shipping container home is connected to a municipal or local grid, then you might be in luck. A lot of perks come with connecting to a grid, starting with continuous access to electrical energy. In such a connection, though, the final touches must be done by an electrician and the installation of the meter needs to be under the supervision or at least with approval from the power company. With a shipping container home, you probably will install that power meter on the exterior walls, though more sophisticated options can work with no need for someone to come and take the reading. Still, the visibility of a meter is always required even if that is the case.

If you have another property next to the container home (like a residential home), you can take advantage of that because the other property will be connected to the grid. You can connect from that property's electrical lines to the container home, which is great since a DIY approach will work fine here. You can use a flexible cable designed for outdoor use to add this extension to your residential electrical installation.

Off-Grid

Off-grid installation means you will be using solar, wind, or hydropower sources to provide electricity. Those solutions are better for the environment and they save a ton of money on utility bills, though they might have downsides; the power that you get might not be sufficient for all your needs. It is a valid option, and a lot of shipping container homeowners prefer these alternative means of energy since they are cheaper and more environmentally friendly.

The great thing about off-grid electricity sources is that it all is up to your discretion. There are no dealings with power companies or energy bills (and no power meter). This independence is important for people who want to live off the grid and homesteaders. Be careful though because this doesn't mean you don't have codes and regulations to follow. Even off-grid power sources have certain codes and requirements. While those systems invite DIY approaches, you will most likely need outside help because installing those systems might be complicated. Converting your direct current power that comes from solar energy, for example, to the high voltage you need to power appliances is tricky and is not something you can do without an expert's help.

The Wiring

Installation of pipes for power line

Interior/Exterior of the Container

1. Conduit

The first part of the container home's interior wiring is the conduit. This is the tubing around the exposed wires to protect them from wear and tear due to humidity, water, and any other external factors that might jeopardize the wire's properties. Conduits are also used to keep wires from freely hanging between the walls, so they route them along selected paths. For a DIY approach, a PVC schedule 40 or 80 conduit is a good place to start and it can provide the necessary protection for just about any wires you plan on using for your shipping container home.

In some places, conduits might be required by the electricity standards of a country or area, but it is generally a good idea to use them even as extra protection and additional security, especially for container homes. Conduits have a dark grey color that helps differentiate them from water pipes, and when installed properly with glued fittings, they are waterproof. This means you can bury them underground without having to worry about moisture seeping into the wires and causing problems. Non-metallic sheathed (NMC) cables such as Romex are not always viewed as the best option in rigid conduits, since this may lead to overheating. Still, no regulations say you can't use NMC with rigid conduits. If you install it properly and choose the right diameter of conduits, there should be no problems.

But flexible conduits don't provide protection against external conditions, but they might be used for routing and can make it easier to upgrade the wiring if you need to.

2. Electric Metal Tubes and Raceways

For the exterior wiring of your homes, a rigid conduit isn't always the best answer. Fortunately, some alternatives are frequently used in the industry and can fix this problem. Electric metal tubes (EMT) are created with an interior coating that makes it much easier and smoother to pull wires. It is also designed to protect the wires against impact and magnetic fields, and there is even a zinc coating on the outside to protect the EMT against corrosion.

One reason why rigid conduits are not a good idea for the exterior of your home is the insulation used. It is often block foam insulation, which means those panels will need to be cut so you can accommodate the conduit. Doing so jeopardizes the thermal insulation and might lead to complications down the line. Another answer to this problem is foam panels designed with raceways specifically added for electrical wiring to go through. Those foam panels often have horizontal and vertical raceways to accommodate any Romex wires you would like to add on the outside of your home. The design is specifically made with the corrugated walls of shipping containers in mind, so it fits the corrugation pattern, while also keeping the thermal insulation efficiently.

Grid Wiring

Connections on the container's interior/exterior aside, you must consider connections to the grid. As we mentioned earlier, maybe your shipping container home is temporary, and if so (and there is a residential home or building next to it), you can use an aerial cable. You just need to find one suited for outdoor use and connect it to the residential network, but keep it above ground level.

As for the most common option, permanent containers require a different approach. You need to bury the electric wire in a trench and use a rigid conduit for this connection (schedule 80 PVC is ideal here). For some countries, local authorities' recommended depth is one and a half feet, which is to put it out of gardening depth. If your container home is in a colder area, increase the depth to avoid any external factors jeopardizing the conduit and wiring.

Off-Grid Wiring

While solar or wind or hydro energy wiring might seem like it presents fewer challenges than grid wiring, it is not without its complications. The first thing you need to know is that such systems operate at lower DC voltages. This does reduce the risk of electrocution, but the wiring needs to be executed properly or else you will face other problems and risks. The generator for energy is low voltage, and you need to transfer significant power from this source to power the house, so this entails high currents that not all cables can withstand. With such high currents, heat increases, and if you don't have the right cable, it will overheat and damage the entire system, increasing the risk of fires. These problems are exacerbated because off-grid power sources are usually far away from the home, so the wires are longer; this means that the problem can be spread.

Tips

Turn off the power: Before you do any work with any wiring, always make sure the power is off at the breaker box – a simple task. The risk of electrocution is always high when working with electrical wires. Do everything possible to minimize that risk! This is particularly more important if you have finished the initial building phase and moved on to connecting wires to the grid.

Understand wire colors: Different colored wires indicate their function, so you must understand the functions of the colors so you know what you're working on. For instance, the US has a standard color scheme: black and red are live wires, white or green is the ground wire, and other colors (like blue and yellow) are for switches and other specific purposes.

Never splice: While connecting devices to the electricity grid, some people splice wires if the length isn't enough; you should never do that. If the length isn't sufficient, buy more wire, but never splice the wires during the run itself. Splicing wires should be done only at the fuse box.

Last but not least, enlist the help of an electrician. Even if you use a DIY approach to the whole construction process, electricity is arguably the most important and dangerous part of making a shipping container home. Mistakes at this point can be very costly in not just money, but also in lives. So, at the very least, hire an electrician to tie up the wiring to the grid and finish the wiring for you. It will prove much safer and significantly more efficient than if you do it yourself.

Plumbing

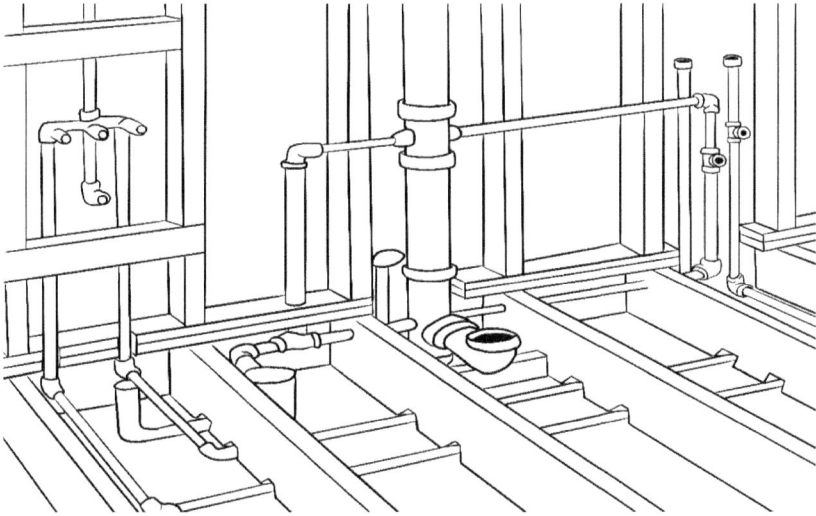

Next on your list of utilities is the plumbing, which includes both water and sewage pipelines. Like with electricity, you will need to have a plumbing plan that outlines the pipes' locations bringing water into the container home and the pipes taking waste out of it. Check your local requirements to discover if you must submit a water plan to construct a shipping container home. If so, it would be a good idea to have an engineer or a contractor draw it up for you since these plans are intricate and require experience to be done properly. Here's how you can have the plumbing installed in your shipping container home.

1. Identify the Main Lines

The first thing you need to do is identify the main water and sewage lines that most likely run under the location you are building your shipping container home. This is a delicate process, and the last thing you need is accidentally hitting a water line while looking for it, or worse, a sewage pipe. So, it is best in this step to enlist the help of water company contractors or an engineer to help you locate the main lines running under your house and mark those locations because this is where you will connect the pipes coming in and out of your house.

2. Make Room in the House

This whole process is obviously done early in your construction phase. You need to drill a hole in your shipping containers' floors in the location in which you plan on installing the plumbing lines. Making these pathways needs to be done carefully so you won't jeopardize the container's structural integrity. Then, remove any debris and dirt after drilling and work on finding the main lines through the hole, but be careful not to break the water pipe while doing so. Once you find the main pipelines, make room around them and this is where you will make the connections.

3. Have the Water Line Shut Off

After making room for the connections to the main lines, contact the water company and have them shut off the water supply so you can install the connection. Then cut into the main water pipe and securely connect your water lines. Do this right to avoid having leaky connections!

After that, take your pipe connection and pass it underground through the shipping container home so you can connect the lines to your different outlets. Don't forget to cover up the area you have dug up when you located the pipelines.

4. Make the Internal Connections

Now that you have secure pipelines running into your shipping container home, it is time to make the connections. Connect the plumbing lines to sinks, toilets, and any other water outlets in your house. Make sure that every outlet leads into the main drain eventually, leading to the main plumbing line underneath the house.

5. Inspection

These pipe connections and fittings need to be done properly and to code, and you should arrange for inspection before you finish. Taps and all pipes need to be working perfectly, and the drain should lead directly to the main lines with no leakage. Make sure the water is draining normally from all sinks, toilets, and bathtubs with no clogging or leaking.

Installing the Pipes

You need to place the pipes running through your shipping container home properly, and this starts with the water plan. It should include the location of all connections and the routes that the pipes will take. Usually water pipes should be installed in the back of the house and underground so they can be protected from breaking or other external factors that might damage them.

An important fact that you need to know is the difference between water and sewage lines and what drives both. Pressure for water lines is responsible for the stream of water for showering or washing. As for sewage lines, it is gravity since the waste flows downward until it reaches the main sewage line. Why is this an important piece of information? Since water lines are pressure operated, if the pipes go upward, it will not be a problem. But for sewage pipes, they need to have a downward slope so gravity can factor in and allow the waste to flow down to the main sewage line. It is generally recommended to dig the same trench for both water and sewage lines, though.

Usually, water companies and engineers will recommend using PVC piping for water and sewage lines; there are other options, though, depending on your preferences and budget, like copper tubing. You need to secure those pipes coming into and out of your container using small metal hooks and a steel cable that will ensure they won't move or sway with the wind.

Notes on Connections

Bathroom: The bathroom obviously uses more water than the rest of the shipping container home, which you need to consider in your design. The size and locations of sinks, toilets, and bathtubs also play a factor here and you need to consider them because you are designing in a constrained space. A good idea is placing the shower close to the main water supply since it uses up a lot of water. This will shorten the distance the water travels and give you better flow.

As for toilets, you need to invest in a good toilet system for your shipping container home. The connection needs to be strong and durable. A good inflow and outflow for the toilets aren't exactly luxuries, but you need to invest in doing this right.

Sewage: For plumbing, sewage is the part that has to be done impeccably, or else you could face health hazards and other problems. The waste coming in from sinks, toilets, and bathtubs needs to be disposed of cleanly and safely to keep a healthy environment. While the most common option is connecting your sewage lines to the main sewage, some people go for separate biodegradable septic tanks to manage their waste.

General Tips

Make sure the water lines are at least fourteen inches away from any electricity, phone, or sewage lines to avoid having any disasters should a pipe leak.

Keep the bathrooms and kitchen as close as possible to the main drain in your design. This ensures the highest efficiency when it comes to plumbing, though that option might not always be accessible if you are going for multiple floors for your house.

Telephone Lines

Water and sewage lines often run together in the same trench, and the same can be said of electric and phone lines—you can run all four in the same trench if you do it right. Telephone lines should be buried in the ground. You need to drill a hole through the container to run the telephone line. The easiest approach is just to connect it to the telephone jack and you're good to go.

Remember that you will need to set up the telephone line for raft and trench foundations first before pouring the concrete. There, you can run a PVC pipe through the concrete so you can pull the phone lines later.

Chapter 7: Roofs

Working on the Roof

Roofing is an integral part of the design process, and the good news is you have a lot of options here. After your container is delivered, you can work on the roof to fit it however you want. The easiest and cheapest option you've got is to use the roof that the shipping container already comes with. But this is far from ideal. Leaving the container's roof as is will invite problems like pooling water, rust, and the inability to control the heat inside the container without proper insulation. Shipping container roofs are made of steel, and in summer, this could turn the entire thing into a furnace.

The good news is you can change the container's roof according to your preferences, and you have a ton of options here. We will explore these options and what you can do with each.

1. Flat Roof

As we just mentioned, the flat roof that already comes with the container is the cheapest and fastest way if you are on a tight budget. The great thing about this roofing option is that you can change it later on or add another roof. A flat roof is durable, and it could last your shipping container home for years, so it is not exactly a short-term solution. Another good feature of flat roofs is that they require little modification to be kept as is, but you must minimize the damage that could happen to them due to external conditions.

Water pooling: The first problem you might encounter with a flat roof is the pooling of water, leading to rust and a host of other problems that will compromise your roof's structural integrity. To prevent that from happening, you can add tarpaulin to cover the roof of your container, and then supplement it with asphalt rolls to weigh the tarpaulin in place and provide an extra layer of security. To keep the asphalt rolls in place, leave an overhang of about two inches in place while covering the roof. Then, bolt two-inch steel bolts into the container from the top through the asphalt, and seal any space around the steel with mastic to avoid leakage if it rains.

Remember to add insulation before doing all this. Cover the roof with insulation like spray foam and then add the tarpaulin and asphalt. This will provide a much needed additional layer of security and insulation if anything goes through the tarp and asphalt.

2. Shed Roof

A shed roof is the sloped roof is a great option if you want to covert the roof of your shipping container home. The great thing about this particular roof is that it is very cheap to make and it is also simple. The whole process of making a shed roof could take a few days and you can then install it over your shipping container home. Shed roofs also work well with solar panels and make it easier to use solar power, if that is the energy source you choose. This is because angling the solar panels toward the sun gives maximum solar radiation exposure.

Another great benefit to a shed roof is how it prevents water pooling due to its slope; it's a good idea to make that slope angled away from the front entrance of your home to prevent water puddles in front of your door. So, make that slope angle to the backside of your home by making one side of the container the high end of the slope, and the opposite side the low end of the slope.

To install a shed roof, you will need a few tools and some skills with them. It is much easier compared to other types, but you need to do it precisely so the roof won't be compromised. So, how do you install a shed roof?

Structure of the Roof

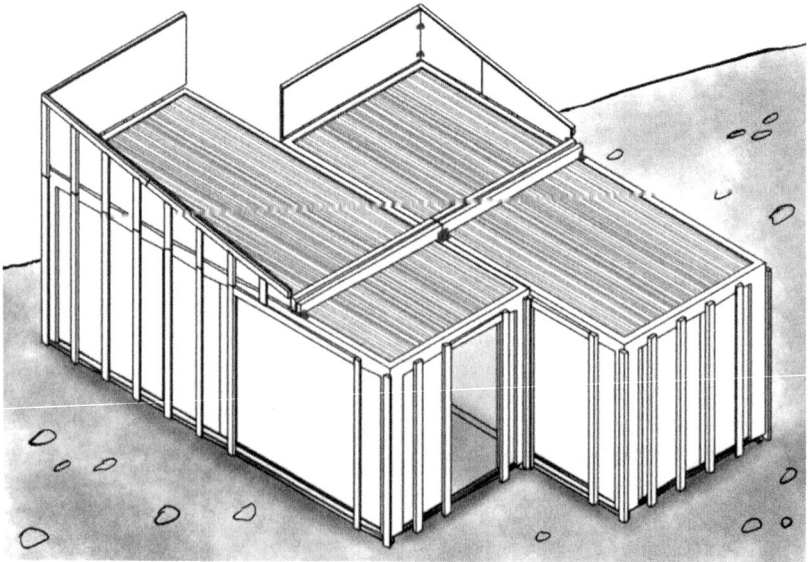

Structure cover count

The first thing you need to do is weld right-angled steel plates that span the shipping container's length on both sides—the main purpose of those steel plates is to anchor the shed roof to the container, so this is not optional. On those steel plates, add wooden beams on each side of the shipping container roof, and then screw the trusses into that wooden beam. This is when the roof's skeleton takes shape. Then, you need to add structural support to the trusses to stabilize the roof's structure. You can attach steel bars or purlins across the trusses. Don't forget to add braces to the trusses to protect them against wind loads.

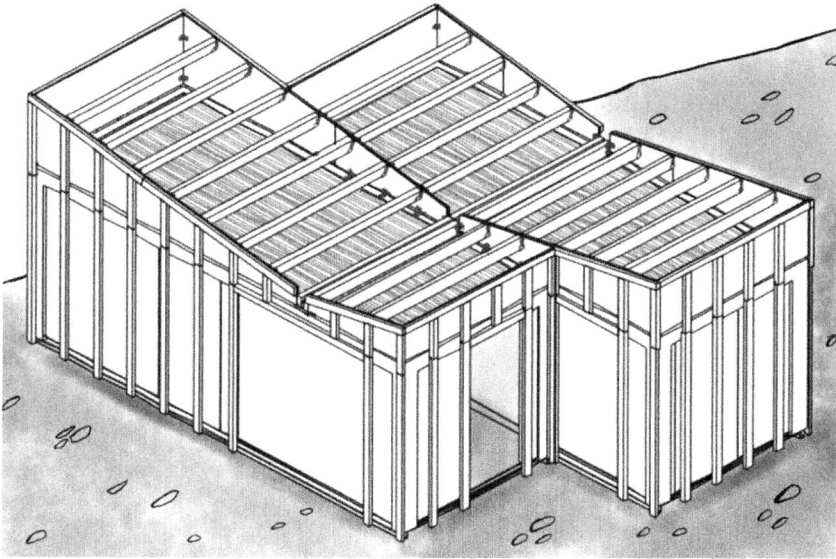

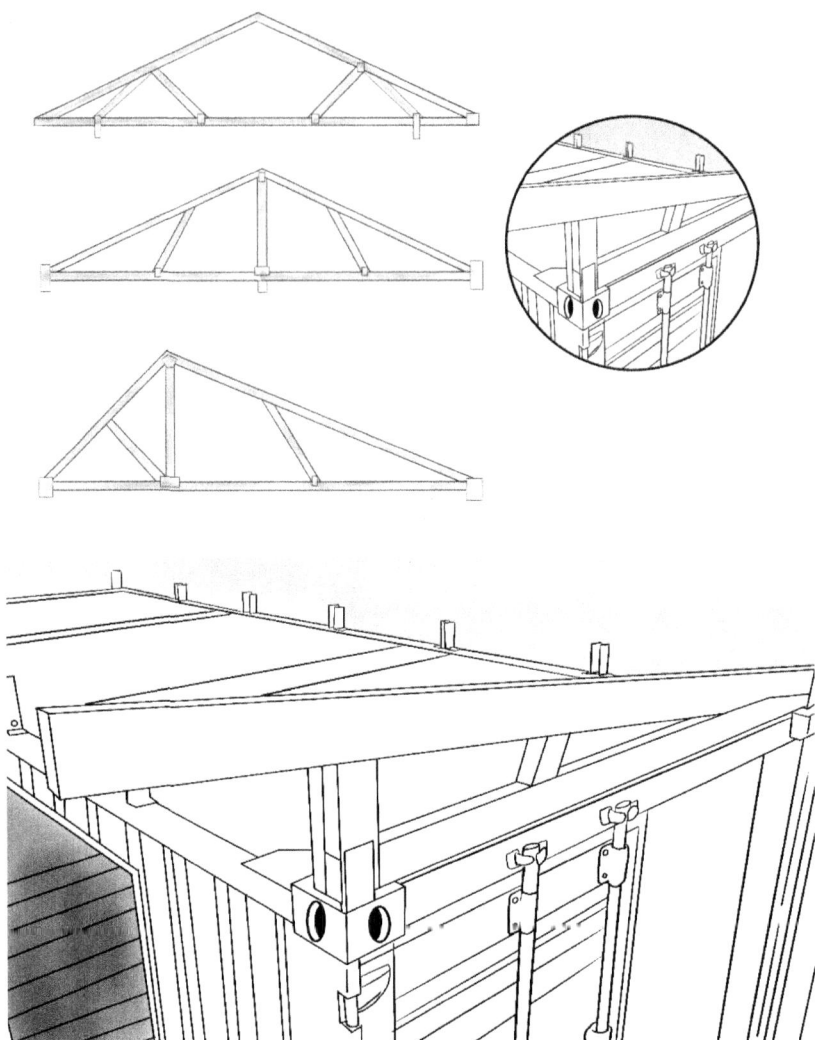

General tips: You should add the trusses at a spacing of eighteen inches, which adds up to about 14 trusses for a 20 ft. container and double that for a 40 ft. container. The trusses need to be screwed to the wooden beam using the skew nailing technique, which means pounding on one nail from the right and one from the left or vice versa. Another very important point to remember is the bracing you will use for your trusses, which is related to the loads they will endure like wind, rain, and snow. This is when it is best to consult with a structural engineer who can advise you on the load-bearing requirements in your area.

Covering the roof

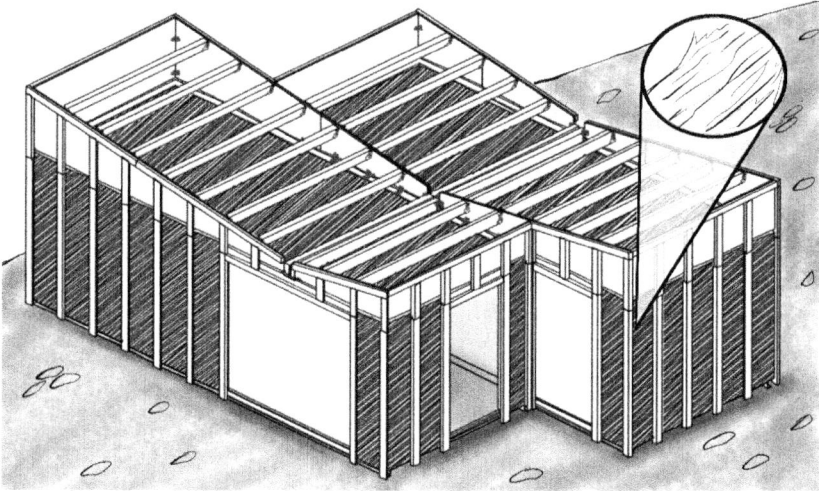

Thermal insulation installation

One great advantage of shed roofs is that you have options with the materials to cover your roof, unlike the container's original one, which is just steel. You can use shingles, coated steel, or galvanized metal sheets. Each type has its pros and cons, and it will be up to you to choose which type you want to go with. For instance, galvanized metal sheets are durable and they're easy to fit around the roof, but coated steel is the most durable, though it is the most expensive option of the three. Shingles is the cheapest choice and they are the easiest to work with, if you don't have outside help or a significant set of skills. The main problem with shingles, though, is that they don't last for long and need constant maintenance.

Ventilation

Whatever kind of roof you go with, you need to make sure that it is properly ventilated. You also do the same with your container's underside by leaving space for the heat and cold to flow without obstruction, so it won't be redirected to your house. To do that with shed roofs, you need to let the trusses overhang your container by one inch. Add a fascia and soffit board under the trusses, and make sure the board has an air gap at its center to let the air to flow in and out of the roof, and cover it with wire mesh to prevent pest infestations.

3. Gable Roof

A gable roof is the type you see at most traditional homes, characterized by its unique triangular shape. It is also a great choice for shipping container homes that comes with a ton of benefits, starting with its excellent water drainage features. Owing to its triangular design with slopes on both sides, a gable roof ensures that no water pools will be formed over the roof of your shipping container home. This reduces the possibilities of any leakage and also extends the lifespan of the roof greatly. People also like gable roofs since they provide more ceiling space than other types. One last perk that comes with gable roofs is that extra space allows for more and thicker insulation, thus controlling the heat much more efficiently in the container home.

The steps to install a gable roof are similar to those of shed roofs. You also start by welding right-angled steel plates on both sides of the roof across the container's length. Next, attach the wooden beams to the steel plates. After that, screw the trusses into the wooden beams and then attach the purlins. Remember to make space for ventilation, so you have to make sure the trusses are overhanging over the container as with shed roofs. Same as before, add in a fascia and soffit board under the trusses for ventilation. Cover the board with mesh wiring to avoid pest problems and to improve the ventilation.

Similar to shed roofs, you can choose from shingles, coated steel, or galvanized metal sheets. They will have the same pros and cons, so the factors affecting your choice are pretty much the same.

One last tip about roofing and its adjustments is to get help from a structural engineer. Even if you plan to do it yourself and have the skills and tools to do it from scratch, you might still need their help, regardless of the roof you will go with. They will help you calculate the load-bearing requirements for your roof, which is basically the combined weight that your roof's structure can withstand without collapsing. This doesn't just mean transient loads like wind, rain, and ice. They will also help you calculate the dead loads acting on the shipping container roof like the weight of the trusses itself, purlins, or roof tiles if you're using them, and live loads such as the weight of equipment and people working on the roof.

These factors are relevant and play into your roof's design, and you need an expert's take on this. Some areas, for example, suffer from high winds, others heavy rain. The design criteria between both cases will be different, and you can't figure out those criteria on your own without the help of a structural engineer.

Chapter 8: The Interior

Working on the Container

So far, you've only worked on cleaning the container, and on the exterior, whether that is the roof or insulation. Now, it is time to get into the interesting part of the construction process. Suppose you have the container as it is without pre-made modifications. There, it will be up to you to work on removing the parts of the walls you don't need, making room for windows and doors, and any other modifications you want to do to convert your container into the living space you have in mind.

This part of the project is when your hands get dirty, and you will need all the tools you can get, from plasma torches to cutting wheels. It would be a good idea to consult with a structural engineer at this point as well to ask about which walls can be removed and what you should avoid to preserve the structural integrity of the shipping container. So, where should you start with converting the container?

Adjoining containers

One of the most common changes that people make while converting shipping container homes is opening up adjoining containers to increase the floor space or make more room. Many people think that working with metal is hard or impossible, but not if you have the right tools and you know what to do. Either way, you must cut through a lot of walls to make room for doors and windows and open up your containers. Cutting through metal might seem daunting, but it is actually easy because, if you do it right, the results can be outstanding and clean. It is a material that can be shaped however you like, which is helpful.

Removing the walls between two adjoining containers only seems logical to increase the living space and make it one big container, considering the tight space that is the interior of a single shipping container. The first thing you need to do is mark and measure the walls you need to remove if you are dealing with multiple containers. It is also a good idea to consider what you want to do with the doors before going to work on the walls. Let's say you have three containers next to each other, for example, will you leave all three doors intact? Or maybe you want to incorporate them into the design somehow. Your last option would be welding them shut and treating them as an ordinary wall.

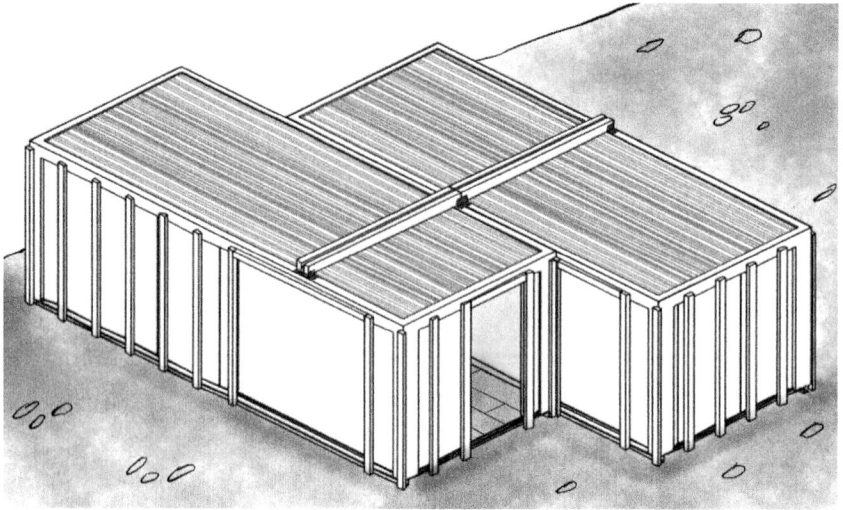

Installation of auxiliary container joining structure

The trick to working on adjoining containers properly is to set them next to each other exactly as you want them to be. If the conversion was done off-site, this will be the only concern you have and the one thing you have to do right. But if you are converting on site, it is a whole other story. Remember to make sure that the containers are well connected to each other with bolts, welds, or clamps before you get to work on the adjoining walls. Then, go to work using a cutting wheel or a plasma torch and remove the wall's space you want to remove. This might be the entire wall or just a part of it depending on your design, which is why you need to measure and mark the parts you want to cut before getting to work.

It would be smart to line the container's adjoining faces with spray foam if you won't be cutting the whole wall, allowing the remaining parts of the wall to have insulation. After cutting the walls, weld steel plates in the gaps between both openings to secure the container walls' structural integrity, but not after spraying the insulation if you hadn't already done it. Then, simply connect the pieces together and finish.

If the conversion was done off-site, you will just have to make sure the openings are aligned and the interior walls are also aligned properly. Having clear plans from the get-go will help you with this part, since you will know exactly where the removed walls will be and how to align the containers accurately. Whether you are converting on-site or off-site, double check your measurements and markings because this is one area where incorrect measurements can be problematic. Also, double-check the steel plate connections between adjoining walls and roofs and make sure there are no loose parts here or there since those can jeopardize the entire house's structural integrity.

Pro tip: Wear protective gear, including gloves, goggles, and/or face shields if possible. Cut metal is sharp and can be dangerous, and you will have your hand around it often in this phase, so you should take safety precautions.

Floors: some people forget to weld the floors after they're done with cutting through the walls. Just as you welded the remainder of the walls with steel plates, you need to do the same with the floors to turn the multiple containers into just the one unit—the last thing you need is walking into your house after it is done to find gaps between the floors. Aesthetics aside, welding the floors together also strengthens your shipping container home's structural integrity and naturally eliminates the chances of any pests sneaking in from the floors or leaks happening.

One last very important detail here is the structural reinforcement if you plan on removing large chunks of the adjoining walls. In that case, you need to use steel box beams to support the load coming from the roof and ceiling, and they need to run across the width of the containers in which you have made those large cuts. Stitch-weld the steel beams to the interior of the container roof. As always, consult with a structural engineer here to tell you exactly the bearing loads that need to be supported by the beams so you can understand which kind to get and of what dimensions.

The great thing about dealing with adjoining walls is that you have a lot of options here. Many container homeowners like to create archways between the two adjoining containers, which increases the space and looks elegant and gives the illusion that the floor space is bigger than it actually is. If archways aren't your thing, you can separate the wall between adjoining containers into segments, with some leading to rooms and others leading to a shared living space, for instance. The possibilities are endless and making changes through adjoining walls is easy enough to give you that flexibility.

Doors and Windows

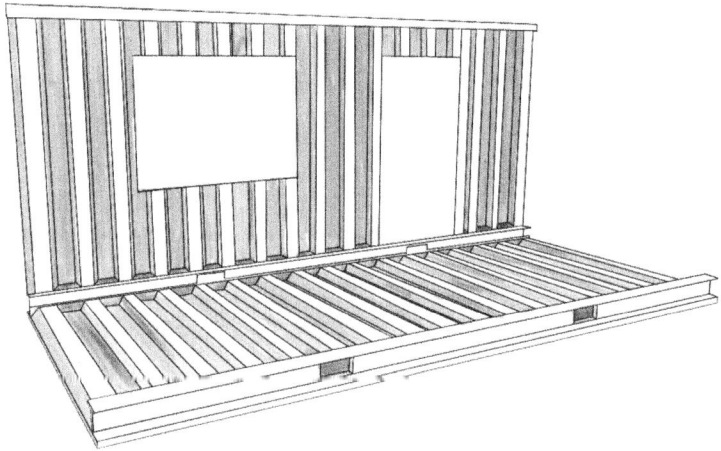

With the walls now open between the containers, your shipping container home should be taking shape quite nicely. Next, you need to start working on the doors and windows and the frames you need for each. The first step to working on windows and doors is taking their measurements and marking their locations on the walls. As always, these measurements need to be accurate and they have to be double-checked because you will be changing the frame of the container, so you can't afford to make any mistakes here. Some experts recommend using cardboard templates for all the doors and windows you will be working on and marking those. Get it right the first time.

Then, cut through the container walls following the measurements you've taken for the doors and windows. Use plasma torches, cutting wheels, and whatever tools you find necessary to do the job. Also, as with converting the walls, remember to wear protective gear because those cut parts will be sharp and can injure you if you are not careful. Make sure all rough edges are smoothed and fill any gaps in the metal walls with a sealant to ensure that your shipping container home is watertight and won't allow pests in. What comes next is creating the frames for the doors and windows, and after that, you install the doors and windows and hang them to the frames.

Making the Openings

To make the openings for walls and frames, the process is pretty much the same as cutting through the container walls to make more space, which we discussed earlier. Like before, take accurate measurements of the required opening and mark it on the container wall. As we mentioned earlier, you can use a cardboard model of the window (don't forget to include the frame) which will help you get exact measurements. Then, cut through the walls with a torch or other tools.

A plasma cutter is probably the best tool to use here because it gives the cleanest lines and the steel you cut can be reused, unlike other tools that might damage that spare steel. If you can't get your hands on one, or you don't know how to use it, you can make do with an angle grinder which will do the job, though managing that tool is complicated because it doesn't easily make straight lines, so you must be patient. Last but not least, use a flap disk to smooth the edges and the opening.

How to Make the Frames

Before you can install the doors and windows, you need to make the frames, which will make your container pop and look like a real home. You can either order prefab frames designed for doors and windows, or you can make them. You could make a square out of galvanized steel tubes with 50 x 50 mm dimensions and cut several lengths of it for the frame. After that, put the frames against the doors and windows to make sure that the measurements are correct. If they fit, remove the doors and windows and stitch-weld the frame. For aesthetics and extra protection, smooth the constructed frame, and then spray-paint it with galvanized paint to resist corrosion.

Now, you have your openings and your frames, so you can weld the frames to the container after cleaning the edges and making sure they are smooth. After that, it is time to hang the doors and windows.

How to Install Doors and Windows

After welding the frames to the opening you have already made, installing the doors and windows is time. Next, hang your walls and windows into the fixed frames and weld them together. You can also use self-tapping screws here to secure the windows and doors in place if you are not handy with welding, though welding is a more durable option and requires less maintenance in the long run. Remember to fill any gaps between the frames and the container with a sealant to maintain its structural integrity—pay special attention to the corners because they are the weakest part of the frame. You should repaint any metal parts with galvanized paint because they might become exposed during the installation process.

Chapter 9: Flooring

A question that many people ask when dealing with shipping container homes is whether they should remove the existing floors of the shipping containers and add in new ones. You can keep the original floors if you want, and it is definitely the cheapest and easiest route to take. The main problem with keeping the original floors is safety. As we mentioned a couple of times in the book, shipping containers often transport materials that might leave chemical residue behind that gets attached to the wooden floors. Moreover, the hardwood floors of shipping containers are usually treated with intense pesticides, and the chemicals in those might threaten people living in the container, which is why you should replace the plywood floors.

You might think that you could look for a shipping container with untreated flooring, but you likely will not find any. The average shipping container is designed to survive long-distance travel in the sea and they have to keep the shipment safe during those trips. The problem is that shipping container plywood floors are made from tropical hardwoods that attract many pests, which is why they need to be heavily treated with pesticides. While this is not a problem if the container is used to transport goods, you plan to use it as a residential home.

Can you order new?

The only way you could avoid this whole pesticide problem is by ordering new shipping containers. If so, then you need to request that the plywood floors are not treated with pesticides. You could even try ordering shipping containers with different flooring types instead of plywood like bamboo or steel, but that might cost more.

Still, the fact is, most people don't order new containers but build their container homes with used ones, and if you have any intentions of keeping the original plywood floors, you need to discover what chemicals they have been treated with. Fortunately, you can find that data on the consolidated data plate that is usually attached to the container's front side. There is a section called 'timber component treatment' on the plate, and on it, you will find the chemicals used to treat the plywood floors.

You will need to do a bit of research here. After learning the chemicals used to treat the container's wooden floors, check the World Health Organization's classification of pesticides so you understand how bad the chemicals are for humans. It is worth noting, though, that the information you find on the data plate will just concern the chemicals used to treat the floors. It will not include whether the container previously transported shipments with chemical materials or if any harsh chemicals were spilled on the floors. So, there is always the possibility that the floors already contain worse chemicals than pesticides.

Replacing the Plywood Floors

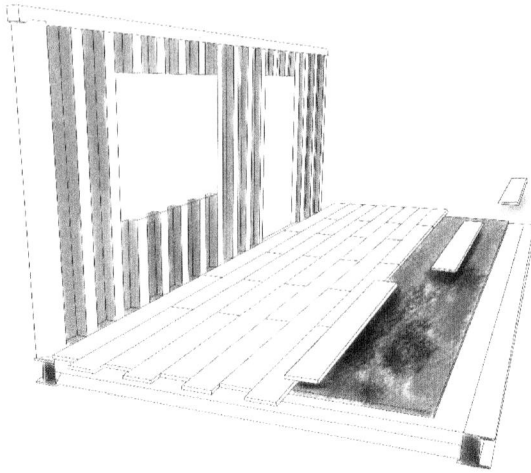

Do you have to remove the plywood floors and replace them? No, you don't. Is it a good idea? Yes, it definitely is. Different factors play into this decision, starting with your budget, but most people remove the original shipping container plywood floors and replace them with new floors just to be on the safe side. It certainly is the safest option, and you won't have to worry about the kind of chemicals that might be lingering in the wooden floors. So, assuming you want to go forward with this, how can you remove the existing plywood floors?

Removing floor bolts. you need to start by cutting the floor bolts first. You can use a handsaw or a reciprocating saw, whichever you have in your toolbox. Locate the floor bolts first; you will find them at 12-inch spacing along the cross members. Do this step delicately to avoid damaging the container's underside and, more important, wear protective goggles.

Removing the floor: Next, get a pry bar and remove the floor panels by forcing them up and then toss them out of the container. There isn't much to this task, but it could take a lot of time, especially if you're dealing with a 40 ft. container rather than a 20 ft.

one. After removing the existing floors, you can add in the new ones.

Insulate: the great thing about getting rid of the plywood floors is that it makes it a lot easier to apply insulation to that part of the container. Normally, isolating the container's underside is tricky, and it has to be done when a crane is lifting the containers. But when you remove the floor, you have access to the floor's cross members, so you could apply spray foam or panel insulation here before adding in the new floors.

Then you can install any kind of floor you want. The underside of the container is insulated, the chemically laced plywood floors are removed, and all that is left is for you to add in the new floor.

Keeping the Plywood Floor

As we mentioned earlier, you don't necessarily have to remove the plywood floors if you don't want to do it, but there are some things that you should do to minimize the risks. Here's what you can do.

Remember that you can add waterproofing sheets before adding subfloors or anything else to ensure that your floors' permeability is minimal, as shown in the below diagram.

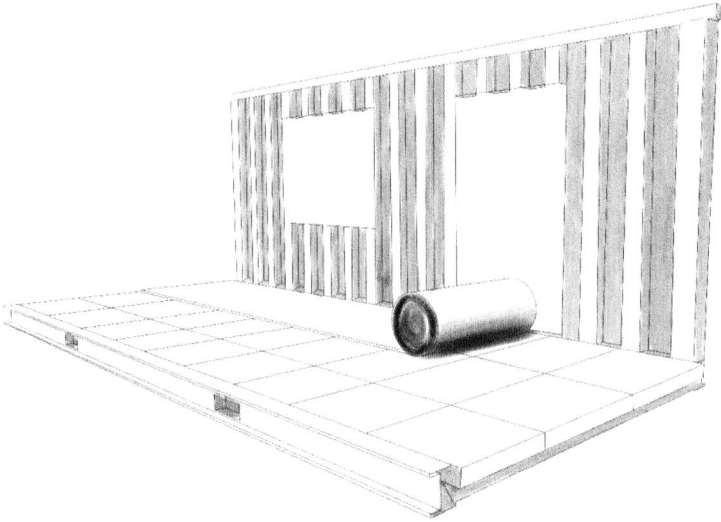

1. Install Subfloors

If the existing plywood floors aren't seriously damaged, and you want to keep them, you can add a subfloor. This will help you avoid the hazard of any possible chemicals that might be lingering in the plywood seeping into your living space. To ensure that those chemicals on the floor are contained, you first need to seal the floor. Start with cleaning the existing plywood thoroughly, you can use isopropyl alcohol for that task. Then, add a coat of low viscosity epoxy, which has excellent abilities to contain moisture and works perfectly in damp conditions. One epoxy coat is usually enough to seal the floor, but you can use two to be extra sure.

Leave the epoxy to dry so it can contain any harmful vapors that might be leaking from the original floor. It would be good to add a layer of foam insulation to provide even more insulation to the entire house. Then install a layer of marine plywood over the layers of foam and epoxy. After that, drill through the new and original plywood layers with screws to fix in the new floor.

2. Treating the Original Floors

If adding a subfloor isn't something you are interested in, and you'd just like to keep the original floor as is, then you will need to treat it first. As we mentioned earlier, the risk with the original plywood floors of the containers lies in the fact that they might emit hazardous vapors and fumes, whether from previously added pesticides or shipments. To get rid of those fumes, you need to contain them. For that purpose, we will also use epoxy here. It is the perfect sealant for this case, and it will stop any fumes from seeping into the rest of the house. You'll also want to clean the floor with alcohol before adding the epoxy.

3. Concrete

This is another option you have if you want to keep the original flooring. The great thing about concrete is that you will not need to add epoxy to seal in the floor or add a subfloor. You will just pour the concrete directly on the original plywood floor, and it will create a natural sealant layer when it dries. The concrete can also be the finished product, so this will be the floor you will use around your shipping container home.

A lot of perks come with using concrete for the floors. It is easy to clean, it is quite durable, and can last for quite a few years. You can also work with concrete and make the design yours. It can be dyed if you want to change the color or polish it and give it a shiny finish. The downside of using concrete is it absorbs cold, so it might be colder during wintertime. Another downside to using concrete is that it requires steel enforcement as we mentioned earlier, though this step is not as complicated as you might think. You'll just add steel bars across the length and width of your floors to form a grid, but make sure they are at least an inch higher than the original plywood. Weld them at a distance of one foot from one another and pour your concrete.

Finishing Touches

Adding in new floors or leaving the original one (after treating it) isn't the end of flooring renovations. Get the work done on the container's flooring before you get to work on dressing the interior and framing. After that, it is time to add some finishing touches to the floors. Concrete aside, you can add in tiles, carpeting, or a new laminate layer to cover your floors. Many people choose hardwood floors but those cost more.

One thing you need to consider while figuring out how you want to finish your floors is the weather. In a warmer climate, you don't want a floor that can radiate heat, but rather one that can help you cool down. A great option here is concrete as we mentioned earlier, but you can also use tiles and laminate too. These floors store cold temperature and help keep your living space cool when the weather is hot. One the other hand, if you live in a colder area, carpet is your best choice because it doesn't transfer cold as much as concrete or tiles. The downside to carpeting is that it is a bit more exhausting to clean, but it gives you warmth in cold weather which makes up for that problem.

Adding Tiles

The great thing about tiles is that they are easy to clean and they can come in amazing designs you will love, and they keep the house cool in hot weather. When you place the tiles, the safest bet is placing them along the shipping container's width and length, whose dimensions help make this a lot simpler and you won't need too many special cuts. While you can add in the tiles before or after framing the interior, it's suggested that you add them afterward. Putting the tiles before framing the walls means you must cut the tiles to fit the steel corrugation, but if you do it after framing, you will just cut the tiles as you would with any traditional home.

Placing the tiles might sound easy, but it is a bit trickier than you might think; there is an art to it. You have to know where to start and which pattern you would like to follow because there are quite a few options. You can tile the place from one wall and make your way to the opposite wall, placing them row by row. Or you can start at the center of the container and move from there, which is ideal if you want to set the tiles diagonally or in a certain pattern; still, this approach means you will cut all the tiles that are adjacent to the walls. If you plan to make a pattern or alternating colors, you need to try it out first by arranging your tiles before you start the process. See a mockup of how it would look and what might work and what might not work.

This will also help you work quickly since the adhesive sets pretty fast, so you need to know what you're doing and what tiles go next. In short, prepare before you start setting the tiles in a certain patter, it will save you a lot of time and effort. Some people do tiling for a living, so it might not be as easy as you think, which is why you should keep to a simple pattern if you have never worked with tile.

For the adhesive, you have a few options. You could use either thin-set mortar (a mixture of cement, water, and fine sand) or tile adhesive for floors. The mortar sets in about a full day, and you shouldn't walk or place anything on it until the full 24 hours expire. On the other hand, floor tile adhesive sets much quicker, depending on the type you are using. It is also a lot easier to work with, especially if you are new to all this. The problem with adhesive is that its water-resistance capabilities are not good. It can easily mold if you have high water inflow from a flood, for instance, and will lose its adhesive power. Adhesive also might suffer if there's constant, significant movement on it for extended durations. Thin-set mortar is more durable and has higher water resistance abilities. It's best to use adhesive with vinyl and linoleum, while mortar is best used with ceramic tiles and porcelain.

Be careful while using both mortar and adhesive because they dry up pretty fast, so don't cover large spaces while working. Instead, take it one small space at a time and then place the tiles in the area where the adhesive is. Lay the material and cover as much space as you can work in ten minutes or so. Put the first tile, press on it, and move on to the next one. Always use tile spacers on the corners because they help you keep proper alignment between the tiles and you will avoid small changes in the angles, which can be problematic in the future. Make sure the tiles are properly leveled;

you can use a spirit level for that. Work all the tiles using the same approach.

While it would save you a lot of time directly placing the tiles over the plywood of a subfloor, the tiling might not come out evenly. Some experts recommend adding a layer of concrete over the plywood floor to make sure the surface is smooth and even, and then you can add your tiles, which will ensure a much more even finish. Concrete is also a much better surface to use with mortar or floor adhesive.

Carpeting

If you're living in a colder climate, then carpeting is definitely the best choice, especially if you like to walk around your home barefoot. You can also add in carpet if you like how it looks and feels, and the great thing about carpeting is that it gives you a lot of options in terms of design and aesthetics. The main challenge you will face with carpeting is that it is more cumbersome to clean, but on the plus side, it is easy to place.

You can't just lay the carpet on your shipping container floors, though. You need to first add carpet grippers, thin pieces of wood with pointy pins protruding from one side, to hold the carpet's edges in place. So, add the carpet grippers at the edges of the container or the room you want lined with carpet, and make sure the grippers are either nailed to the floor or safely in place using adhesive. Make sure you leave a small space of 1 cm between the grippers and the walls. Next, the smart thing is to add carpet underlay, which will provide comfortable cushioning and make the carpets a lot easier to walk on. A standard carpet underlay has foam on one side and rubber on the other, and you need to place that latter part down on the grippers and unroll it from wall to wall. Remove any excess underlay by cutting it with a blade. Do the same with any area with carpets and make sure the underlay is comfortably placed on the carpet grippers. Connect any gaps between overlay layers using carpet tape to avoid having any level inconsistencies in your carpet.

Then you can place the carpet you have chosen. Cut the exact dimensions that make the carpet fit comfortably in the room, and do the same with other rooms in the house. While placing the carpet, start at a corner, and make sure it is secured into the carpet gripper. Leave a space of around 2 inches since the carpet will stretch. Once you're done with the first corner, move to the next one along the wall, attaching the carpet to the grippers along the way and fitting it properly. Have a utility knife on you so you can cut off any excess carpet and help it fit perfectly in the room.

Laminate Floors

Laminate flooring is one of the best and most elegant solutions for finishing the floors, but it is best done after framing the house's interior. It is easy to add and you can put it over a subfloor or an overlay, so that certainly makes things simpler. The best way to start with laminate tiles is to start at the far end of the room, placing the tiles from left to right, and working your way until you reach the opposite side—the door. Do the same for each room, but adjust accordingly. It is always best to work from the side opposite the door and work your way until you reach the threshold.

Laminate flooring often comes with tongue and grooves so you can fit each tile into the next one. Slide the one you have in your hand at an inclined angle against the one already placed, lower it, and then comfortably slide it against the tile until it is securely in place. Do the same with all tiles until you finish the first row and do the same moving forward. You might need to cut the last tile in a row so it can fit the space, and you have to get the measurements right with this. Put the new tile over the old one, mark the length you need for it to fit, and cut along your marking and then place it.

Remember that it is always advisable to leave laminate floors until you are done with framing the interior walls, or else you must cut the laminate tiles to fit the corrugation of the steel wall as we mentioned earlier. So, it's always best to frame the walls first so you won't have to spend so much time on this consuming process. Another tip, while working with laminate, it would be smart and alternate the joints; you can do that by using any discarded sections from the previous row and starting with it on the next one. This is important because it ensures that joints would never line up against one another.

Chapter 10: Framing and Ceilings

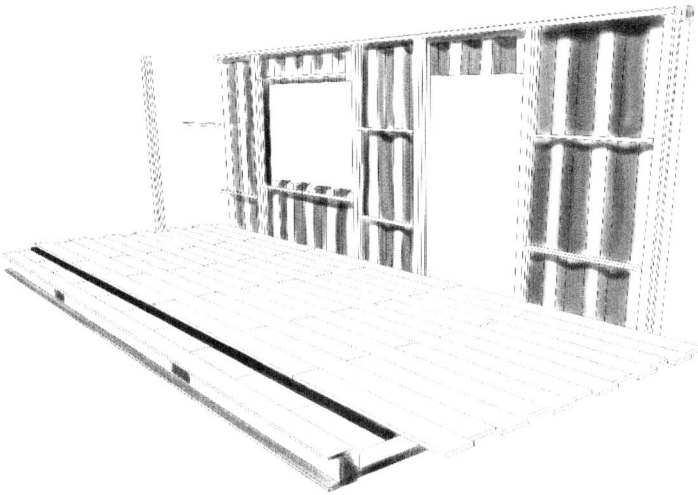

Profile installation

At this point, the shell of your home is pretty much complete. You installed the roof, added windows and doors, and the floor is just about finished. What comes next is transforming the open plan of your shipping container home into separate rooms, also known as framing the house. At this stage, always consult with the plan so you can understand where the interior walls need to be added and how you will separate the rooms. The main function of those walls is to partition the rooms, so you can't add them randomly without checking the plans you have based on the wiring and electrical systems and plumbing and other services.

While most of the work with framing is done inside the house, you could also choose to frame the exterior walls of your home, though that is not a necessity. It will, however, provide further insulation and also a frame for wall paneling or if you wish to hang drywall. It will also give you the chance to work on giving your home a beautiful finish from the outside if you wish. As for the materials used for stud-walls (another name for frames), you can use either steel or wood. Steel will give you about an extra inch around the interior walls, but it is more expensive, and you will also need specific tools to work on it, which might not always be available. Wood is naturally cheaper, but you won't get the additional 1-inch perimeter around your interior stud walls, but that rarely presents a problem.

Interior Walls

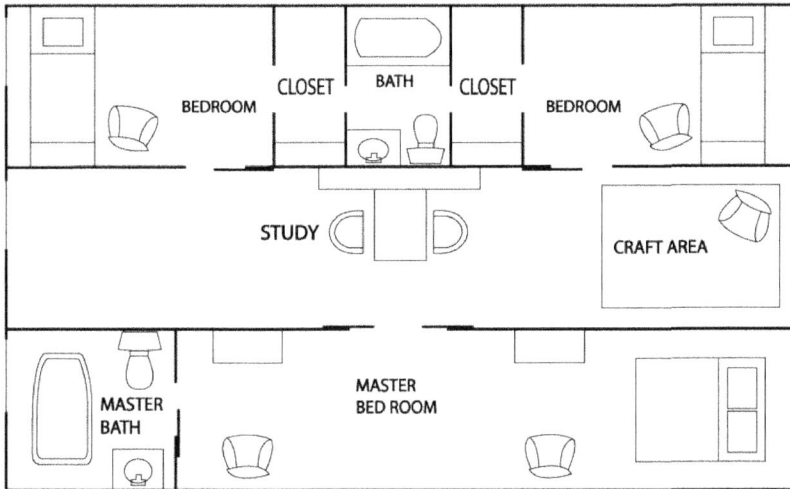

Let's take the plan as an example of the interior framing. Assuming these are two 40 ft. containers, the interior walls in black are the ones that need framing. Any partitioning walls will always need to be framed, but you will also have to cut through the walls during the conversion process to make room for the partitioning walls.

1. Beaming

The average stud wall consists of battens, a head plate, and a sole plate. The first thing you need to do to frame is to set the beams. Head beams take the top length of the wall as opposed to sole beams that run the bottom length of the wall. So, start by setting up the head plates for all the interior walls you will be working on and line those spaces. Use 2 and a half inch self-tapping screws to connect the head plates to the roof, and the sole plate can either be similarly screwed or nailed in place. Make sure the spacing between the nails or screws is equal at around 2 feet. You should do this before adding your finished floor.

2. The battens

After setting up the beams, you need to place the studs or battens. Those take the vertical length of the wall from the head to the sole plate. You can screw or nail the battens to both head and sole plates. Use 5 cm/2-inch nails or self-tapping screws for this process. Either way, the best approach for this is to follow a skew pattern to get the best possible lateral stability. Screw or nail each batten twice at a 25 -degree angle from vertical, which will help increase the walls' resistance to lateral loads. This pattern is done for both the head and bottom of the stud. The best way to go is to start by lining the interior walls of your container, and after that move inward into the partitioning walls separating interior rooms.

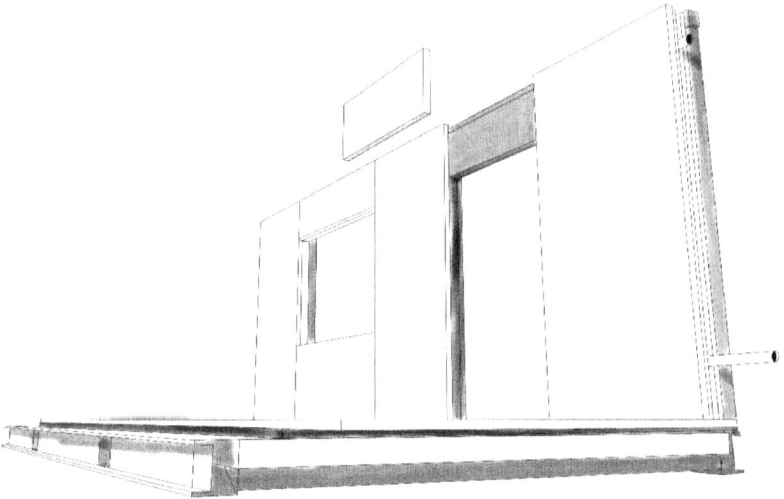

Installation of walls and partitions

Interior Doors

If you're doing interior walls, you probably will have quite a few interior doors within your shipping container home. This is another process where going back to the plan is a must. You will be using this plan in parallel with building the stud walls because every time there is a door, you have to consider it while attaching the interior walls. There needs to be a batten lining on each side of the door and a noggin (horizontal beam) at the top, which lines the top of the door frame and provides support for the wall finish overhanging above the door, too. Also, be very careful not to add in any battens where there will be a door because you need this to be an open space, so again, revert to the plans.

After finishing with the stud walls and considering the doors' location, it is time to hang your internal doors. You will just place them into the frame's opening and nail them once you are certain that they are level. There is also the possibility of purchasing reframed doors, which means you will just hang them in the stud walls' opening. Remember that this setup is ideal for light plasterboard, and the support beams can handle that load. But if you are going to use heavy plasterboard, you will need a bit more reinforcement. Tip: if you are using heavier studs, reduce batten spacing and put them about 1 ft. apart.

If two edges of adjacent plasterboards meet, make sure there is a batten in place there to secure them in place and ensure structural integrity. One point we will discuss in a bit is the ceiling. You can either install a ceiling before or after the stud walls, but each approach will affect the coming steps. If you add a ceiling after framing your shipping container home's interior, you need to attach joists to the roof of your container, and the head plates should be attached to those joists. If you add in the ceiling first, the head plates will be directly attached to whatever material you chose for your ceiling instead. This isn't the better option, and it might not work with some designs, which is why it is better to frame your container first and then add the ceiling.

Installing a Ceiling

Installing a ceiling, much like installing a roof, is a personal choice depending on your personal preferences. You don't have to put one in, but it will certainly make the place look a lot fancier and more to your style. However, an exposed ceiling also has its perks because it shows the nature of your shipping container home, so it might have an aesthetic appeal of its own. Still, adding a ceiling gives room for more insulation and thus better heat/cold control, and it might even provide you with storage space. As we mentioned earlier, adding the ceiling before or after the stud walls is also a matter of choice, but you should do it after framing the walls. You have a few options with ceilings, starting with keeping the original one.

Exposed Ceiling

An exposed ceiling means leaving the container's original one, which, as we mentioned, goes to show the work that went into this home and making it what it is. It will also provide you with additional height since there aren't any additions. Exposed ceilings are a favorite for DIY enthusiasts since it entails saving a lot of time and money. But know that it means less insulation, so you might be paying that money and more in utility bills during winter and summer. Rust and mold might present as problems down the line due to condensation seeping to the roof from the house's interior, but it shouldn't be too serious, and you can fix such problems easily if they occur.

However, it is not recommended to skip out on the ceiling if you didn't add in an additional roof. Keeping both the original roof and original ceiling means you will have little insulation, if any, which can be quite problematic for a shipping container home. So, suppose you don't want to add a ceiling to the interior of the containers. There, it is definitely a good idea to add an additional roof on the outside so you can increase the insulation and dampen the effects of the sun hitting the roof all day long. The better option would certainly be to add a ceiling to the interior of your container. If that is not an option, then you should at least ensure that you have an additional roof.

If you don't want to leave an exposed ceiling, you need to install a new ceiling. Here's how you can start.

There are a few different ways to install a ceiling in your shipping container, but installing joists to the roof is the best way to go. Use two-and-a-half-inch self-tapping screws to connect the joist directly to the roof of your container. As we mentioned earlier, another way to go is to nail the joists into the head plates if you frame your house first. To save a few inches of space for insulation, you should start by attaching the joists directly to your container's roof beams, but this obviously needs to be done before framing the container and adding stud walls. You can then attach the head plates to the joists after framing the ceiling if you do this.

Make sure the joists are placed with 1.5 inches between their centers, which will give you more than enough room for insulation. You can then add insulation between the joists to further improve the insulation of the container. After that, add panels or drywall over the joists and screw it in place.

Finishing Interior Walls

By now, you have framed the interior of your container, added insulation, and come closer to finishing work on your beautiful shipping container home. The shipping containers should be taking shape pretty nicely now, and you can move on to the next step, finishing work on the interior walls. If you look at your inner walls now, you have battens everywhere, and while they don't look bad, the place looks like it's a construction site. This is why the first step in finishing the work on the interior walls is hanging drywall or beautifully designed wood panels that can give your place the feel of a home for the first time since you started this project.

The great thing about this part of the project is that it is fun, and you also have a lot of options to work with. You can start by hanging drywall, and if you did all the right things in the design process, this part should involve minimal cutting. So, lift the drywalls and hang them so their ends can be fixed to the battens. You can use hardwood if you want, and it will be directly attached to the battens.

Covering the Battens

The goal is to eventually cover the battens to improve your shipping container home's overall look and prepare the drywall for paint if you want to do so. You need to cover the battens with the drywall or wooden panels, whichever you want. The best way to add panels or drywalls is at windows and doors and then move outward toward the opposite walls. Ensure the drywall or panels are staggered horizontally to avoid having the seams end up on the same batten, leading to cracks in a few years and other complications.

You should also place your panels or drywall so it lines up with the batten center. It might not be easy to do so around openings like doors and windows, but this will work if you put a little effort into it. Each board you affix needs to be properly attached from all angles. Screw the boards through the battens, head and sole plates, and the noggins. Place your screws at a distance of 8 inches from one another. Repeat the same steps in both vertical and horizontal directions until you are certain the board is attached properly.

When working with plasterboard, it is always recommended to use screws specifically designed for that purpose. Plasterboard screws are usually coated with phosphate and come with a countersunk head. Also, when you are trying to install plasterboard or hardwood panels in your shipping container, you will face awkward spaces, which means you will need to do some cutting. So, measure your board, mark it (use spirit level), and then cut through the board and install it in the space while making sure it fits perfectly with the edges.

Finishing the Walls

The next logical step will be painting over the drywall you have hung. You have a lot of options here, and some people might just hang hardwood panels and be done with it. But most will prefer to paint over the installed drywall for aesthetic value and to give the walls a beautiful finish. You might think that since the drywall is in place, you can get to work and start painting, but that isn't always the case.

Painting over the drywall directly might cause visible protrusions in places and depressions in others around the screws. While more recent plasterboard companies have tried addressing this problem by designing drywall that doesn't necessarily highlight these surface levels, it is always best to add a layer of plaster over the drywall. This will make it much easier to paint over and even the surface, plus give an added layer of protection for the wall.

You can paint without plaster, assuming you're using newer models of drywalls, but in that case, it would be smart to fill the screw holes and any other gaps with a jointing compound. You can use a dedicated filling knife to add the compound into the small holes and make sure you even the compound as much as possible to avoid having anything protruding while you paint. You might also find some gaps between drywall panels along the walls, and those can be sealed with joint tape along the edges. After that, you're ready to paint.

As we mentioned, you have a couple of options here to finish work on your walls. While some people will choose paint, others will go for wood veneer or textured plaster, depending on personal preference. Here are your options to finalize the walls.

1. Painting

After preparing the walls for painting, it stands to reason that you would paint the walls. The drywall is ready, and you can add plaster and start painting. For shipping container homes, lighter colors are always the better choice because they will make the space look bigger than it really is and open up the place. One of the best features of painting is the fact that it is cheap, and it doesn't take up too much time. A few people working on a two-container home can do the job in a couple of days. So, here's how you can start painting the drywall of your shipping container home.

Clean: the first thing you need to do is clean the space and get rid of anything that you don't want to be covered in paint. Remove tools and any other junk that might obstruct you from reaching the walls. And make sure the walls are also dust-free, so wipe them off beforehand with a damp cloth and leave them to fully dry.

Protect the rest of the home: Needless to say, painting can get messy, and unless you want your newly installed floors to get covered in splatter, you should cover the floors and any other parts you won't be painting. Put drop cloths on the floors for any spillage or paint drips. Also cover doors, windows, electric sockets, light switches, doorknobs, and any other part of the home you want to keep protected from the paint.

Understand Paint: Painting isn't simply finding a color you like, getting a couple of cans, and going to work on the walls. There are a lot of things you need to cover and to understand about paint. Ask around about the best color of paint for your shipping container home. The brushes or rollers you will be using will depend on the type of paint or its use. For instance, water-based paint needs synthetic brushes, while oil-based paint can only be used with natural brushes.

Preparing the paint: After getting the paint and the right tools to use with it, you can start to work. First, if you are using more than one can of paint, make sure you mix them all together in a bigger bucket or tub so you can get the same color across the walls. Shake the paint before you use it and mix it using a piece of wood. Pro tip: Close doors and windows if you're working in damp conditions because moisture can be harmful to the paint.

Top to bottom: a tip you'll get from any professional painter is to work your way from the top to the wall's bottom. If you have installed a ceiling, and you want to paint it, then start with it. Then work your way down to the floors. Be careful to cover the walls and ceiling joints with tape if you are using different colors for both to avoid having them mix where you don't want.

After finishing the ceiling, work on the walls, also working your way from top to bottom. If you are painting the walls with a roller, make sure your strokes are long and from the top down. To ensure consistency in color and thickness, put your roller stripe halfway between the previous and following stripes. Also, don't go for thicker layers; rather, apply a few thin ones for consistency and a gorgeous finish. If there are areas with painter's tape, remove the tape and use brushes to fine stroke the last remaining parts, but be careful not to go over the edges.

2. Wood Walls

Fortunately, if painting isn't your cup of tea, you have a lot of other options. You can put real wood walls instead of installing drywall for painting. This means that the wood will be placed over the stud walls, but you need to first add Visqueen to cover the stud walls and their insulation. Nail the Visqueen to the stud walls after stretching it out all over the wall, and only then can you add your real wood finish. The great thing about using real wood for your finished wall is that you have a ton of options here.

One of the best ways to go is to use tongue-and-groove pine slats, which are placed against the studs, but you will work your way from the floor to the ceiling here, unlike painting. Make sure the joints are staggered and that the slats are fixed to the studs. The process isn't complicated, though it will most probably take you more time than painting. Make sure you've measured any excess length for each board so you can cut it accordingly, especially for the final row.

The great thing about real-wood wall finishes is that they give a rustic feeling to the shipping container home and it will feel like a cabin in the woods. It is also a very simple finish to make and it is one of the most visually impressive, too. This approach also requires little skill, and you can do it with minimal tools and equipment.

While real-wood walls are great, they are a bit on the pricier side. You can try an alternative, like vinyl panels that can be installed over the drywall. The trick with vinyl is you will need to cut it to fit the space of the walls, over the windows and doors, around switches and panels, and so on. Vinyl is great for areas with high moisture like the kitchen or bathroom, especially if it is added with caulk.

Chapter 11: Interior Design Ideas

A) Saving space

Now that you are almost finished with the interior of your shipping container home, maybe it is time to come up with design ideas to make the place look and feel a little bit bigger. While you can add more than one shipping container to maximize your floor space, that is not always an option due to budget restrictions, and sometimes, you just have to make do with what you have. The default for shipping containers is that they are snug, which is why every step you take needs to be calculated, whether it is the style of furniture you will use or the location of that furniture.

In this next part, we will explore design ideas to help you make the most out of the space you have without ever feeling it is too tight. We will also talk about suitable furniture pieces and much more.

1. Mezzanine Floor

Installing a mezzanine floor is one of the best ideas you can make in your shipping container home to save space. It is basically an intermediate floor between the ground and your ceiling, on which you can play around with design ideas to save space. For instance, some people add the intermediate mezzanine floor and turn it into a living space, into which you can add a sofa, hang your TV on the opposite wall, and just chill in your home. Underneath the mezzanine floor, you can put the bed and turn it into the bedroom.

Sure, this takes up a lot of the headspace in a shipping container, but it also saves you a lot of floor space you can otherwise use cleverly however you please. The mezzanine floor in our example allows you to have the bedroom underneath the living room all in the same space. You can even play around with the furniture you use to make the most of the space, so the sofa on the upper floor can fold into a bed, and so on. We will discuss furniture pieces that can help you save space later.

2. Add a Pegboard

Pegboards are a pretty useful item to have around any house, especially a shipping container one. They are excellent for storing smaller items that would normally take up too much closet and drawer space. You can store all your cooking utensils like pans, spatulas, knives, sieves, mashers, and much more if you add the pegboard in the kitchen. Maybe you need space for your art room, so you can hang your brushes, drawing pens, tapes, scissors, or anything you use for your art projects.

Using a pegboard clears up space on desks, in drawers, and around the entire house. You just attach them to the wall, add hooks to the pegboard, and you can start using as your personal storage space however you please. A pegboard can also be used in the garage to store tools and any other place in the house. The great thing about pegboards is that they come in different sizes. You just need to figure out the estimate of the size you need it in, depending on what items you will store there, and then you can go get one of standard size or more than one and use them together.

3. Use Dead Spaces

There often are quite a few dead spaces around an average house, whether it is a shipping container home or a traditional one. With a touch of creativity, those spaces can be used to great effect and they can help you save a lot of space. You can start with the space under your bed. Many people add the bed and be done with it, but the average bed takes up a lot of usable space, which is quite valuable in a relatively small space like shipping containers.

This is why you need to take advantage of that space. There are different ways to go about this. Many beds come with dedicated frames that already contain drawers underneath the mattress, and getting one of those can prove useful. This could even save you the need for a wardrobe in the bedroom because you basically have it underneath your bed, so you could store clothes there.

Another space often underused in houses is under the stairs. If you stacked shipping containers in your design, this means you have at least a second floor, and there will be stairs leading to that floor. There is always space under such stairs to be used if you add a few shelves and get a bit creative. You can store books, kitchen utensils, or anything that needs storing around the house.

These are just examples of spaces around the house that can be utilized if you take time to consider it. If you think hard enough, you are bound to find others that can be leveraged to a greater extent.

4. Fold

One of the smartest, and coolest, ways you can save space in a shipping container home is to fold everything and anything that can be folded. This might seem like a stretch to you, but it has been done often before and many people have invested time and effort in such approaches and they ended up with wonderful homes with properly utilized spaces.

You can basically fold, swivel, or rotate everything in your home when you are not using it – if you design it right. Your bed can be pulled out of a wall and become a full-sized bed. You can have your entire kitchen hidden behind wooden panels that can be folded open. The same goes for storage spaces and sofas. Anything can be folded with the right design. It might not be perfect for everyone, but it can certainly save a ton of space.

5. Install Pocket Doors

To save space in your shipping container home, you must get creative with your interior design ideas, there's no way around it. A great way to play around with the design is by installing a pocket door. A pocket door is similar to a barn door, but the great thing about it is how the door retracts into a hidden space (pocket) in the wall instead of swinging open into the room. This means that the whole wall will be free to use when the door it open.

So, there won't be a door taking up space on either side of the wall, and you can get creative with the empty space, too. You can add furniture adjacent to the door, shelves, or anything. This is why pocket doors are ideal for shipping container homes as they can help you maximize your space.

If you think you have the space for it, you can also install a barn door. It has its own rustic, unique design that looks like an actual barn door, but know that the track holding the barn door is mounted on the wall, so it does take up space, unlike pocket doors. Empty wall spaces prove useful, as we'll discuss in a bit, so unless you like the elegant design of that barn door so much, pocket doors are better.

6. Furniture

The furniture in your shipping container home will play a huge role, not just in making the place look nice, but also in saving space. Every piece you get has to be with careful consideration to the space of your home and whether the furniture piece will help save and utilize space. Invest in multitasking furniture that can serve more than one purpose around the place, thus helping you maximize your floor space.

A great example of multi-purpose furniture is a couch that converts into a bed. If you happen to be living alone in a single-container home, for example, such a couch will be of great use and can save you a lot of space and maximize the living area. Your living room and bedroom could be the same, where you just fold and unfold the couch to change it from a bed into a couch or vice versa. Even if you live with others, a foldable couch is quite useful and can accommodate guests and help make room for many things. Here are different types of convertible couches.

Chaise

A chaise is one of the most elegant additions to any home, and it is very useful in tight spaces despite looking somewhat large. Translated into 'long chair,' a chaise is an extended chair that provides support for your legs, but it is a one-person chair, so it has a short backrest. It might not be perfect for overnight sleep, but it is excellent to rest for a bit or watch TV.

Futon

It not only looks exotic and classy, probably due to its Japanese style, and it also is quite functional. A futon is a mattress that folds across its length, and when you fold it up, it is a sofa. So, you fold it when you want to sleep and then unfold it to an 'L' shape when you want a sofa.

Foldout couch

At first glance, the foldout couch (also known as sleeper sofa) looks like a traditional couch, but there is one major difference. When you remove the cushions of a sleeper sofa, you will find a folded mattress and a frame that can be pulled out to form a bed. The cool thing here is how the cushion you sleep on will differ from the surface of the sofa you sit on.

Daybed

Daybeds look quite elegant in any house, and they also are very functional. The daybed has a regular mattress for sleeping, which has a headboard that you pull out to make the bed. When used as a couch, the headboard is the backrest.

7. Leveraging the walls

One thing you must do to make the most out of your shipping container space is leveraging the walls. We mentioned earlier that you can hang pegboards to utilize empty walls, but there is much more that you can do. You don't have a ton of floor space in a shipping container home to install closets and large cabinets, but you have a lot of overlooked spaces on the walls you can use. Your walls are assets as much as your floor space.

If you happen to do a lot of work from home, then you might need a home office. Needless to say, getting a large desk is not practical and can take up a lot of space. Fortunately, there is an alternative. You can mount a foldable desk to a wall, which is one of the best ways to utilize space in tighter locations. You can use your desk for work or whatever, and after you are done, it folds flat against the wall, saving you room to move around or do anything you want. A foldable desk uses brackets or legs to support it from the underside and wires or chains from the top. You can make use of the space above the desk, too, so you can add a few shelves and put flowers, books, or whatever you want to decorate the area.

Another great use of the walls is adding TV mounts. If you're getting a TV, then it could be sizable, and resting it on a table would just be too space-consuming. Consider other options. You can mount the TV on the wall, and like that, you don't need a table or a stand. The great thing about TV mounts is that they come with a lot of options, and some allow you to adjust the viewing angle as you please so you could view the TV from several angles. In other words, you can use the same TV for more than one space, which saves both time and space around the house.

Last but not least, fans mounted on the wall are another great way to leverage the walls inside your shipping container home. While pedestal fans are great, they take up floor space. Ceiling fans, on the other hand, take up ceiling height in an already limited space. This is why a better choice would be mounting the fans on walls. This gives you the benefits of both ceiling fans and free-standing ones. This naturally saves up space around the living container and gives you exactly the type of cooling you need.

8. Add mirrors

Mirrors open up spaces and make places look much bigger than they actually are. A mirror cleverly installed in a room will give the illusion that the floor space is bigger than it is. This doesn't mean you should go plaster the entire shipping container with mirrors. They come in different designs, and some will work better in certain rooms. So, do a little research and find mirrors that work with your space, adding that reflective surface that makes the rooms look bigger than they are.

These were all ideas of how to make the most out of your shipping container home interior space, but if you noticed, most of these ideas related to walls. From mirrors, pegboards, and mounts to sliding doors, these require some form of interior walls. But what if you want to lessen the partitions inside your home, does that mean you won't be able to enjoy your shipping container home? Hardly. You can separate spaces inside a shipping container home in many ways that don't entail using walls. These options often have their pros and cons. Here are ideas that you can try for wall-free rooms.

Curtains

Curtains are a great choice if you want to separate rooms without walls. You can use hanging fabric curtains, with materials that depend on your preference and the properties of your shipping container home. For instance, if you use a heavy fabric that is also dark, it can stop light from seeping into a room of your choice, and it will also work as a decent sound barrier. On the other hand, using lighter fabrics separates rooms while still letting some light and air in, not to mention sound.

If you want something a bit more hip, you can try beaded curtains. They give a certain style to the place and they are excellent room dividers. The cool thing about those vertical strings with beads on them is how they let a lot of light into the room as well as sound. You can also choose the bead colors and designs as you please, and there are quite a few options to choose from. Some designs even make images when they are hanging, like a bookshelf, plants, artist portraits, and much more.

You could go for something a bit more oriental and add a folding room divider. They look quite elegant and they elevate the décor of any room. The most popular type is the trifold dividers. The great thing about this option is you also get a ton of different designs and materials to choose from, so you will most likely find something that complements your taste and takes the room's style to the next level.

B) Lighting

Lighting is one of the basic pillars of any home. Some people think that lighting only serves to provide illumination to a space, but it is so much more than that. Lighting can take your shipping container home's overall style to a whole new level if you do all the right things. Often, with shipping container homes, it is not just the style that you need to worry about, but also the functionality. You cannot add in old incandescent light bulbs and hope for the best. These are huge bulbs, and they require even bigger fixtures to hold them, and as you know by now, space is valuable and scarce in a shipping container home.

Fortunately, lighting technology has evolved over the years, and we now have LED lights, which provide better and stronger light with a lot less hardware. LED lamps are small, and you don't have to worry as much about the fixture holding the light as you would with older options. Owing to their compact size, LED lamps save floor, table, and ceiling space, allowing you to make the most out of your shipping container space. Most importantly, they eat up little power, which means they save you money on utility bills. With lighting, you have quite a few options for your shipping container home.

Indirect lights: this is a great option for any space, not just a shipping container home. It is elegant, stylish, and gives a different vibe to the whole place. Indirect light doesn't fall directly onto the room or living space you want to light. It bounces off a ceiling, wall, floor, or other objects, so you basically never see the light directly.

When that bounce happens, the light is dampened to beautiful effect.

One of the best ways to create that effect is by using LED strips. They are flexible and easy to move around, so you can put them behind a mirror, library, pictures, or any other location, and they will give that soft glow that makes the whole room look beautiful without that annoying glare. LED strips can also be placed underneath cabinets, around counters, and in other locations you want to light discreetly and elegantly.

Direct light: You could also always go for direct lighting options inside your shipping container home, where the light from the lamp falls directly on the living space. For this kind of lighting, you will need fixtures for your bulbs, as well as switches. There are many options here, whether you want to add lamps or chandeliers, though the latter option is one to think about considering the limited ceiling space in a shipping container home.

You can play around with direct lights by adding spots, desk lamps, uprights lamps, and much more. But when doing the math, consider the floor space of the shipping containers to avoid having the lamps overcrowd the place.

Can-less LED lights: these are a great choice for a house that has low ceiling clearance because they are slim and recessed. While older models of recessed can lights are great, they require a lot of vertical space, around six inches, which makes them less than ideal for shipping container homes. Other models, though, require only two inches of clearance from the ceiling and most of that is tucked away in the injunction box, so the actual light takes around half an inch, which is great to save overhead space in shipping containers.

Matching Colors

One last thing to talk about in the interior design of your home is the coloring. We talked earlier about the paint and the importance of lighter colors in making the place look bigger than it is, but coloring extends beyond the wall colors of your shipping container home. You still have furniture, linens, and a lot of things that you need to carefully select when it comes to the harmony between all items in the house.

The colors of the walls and furniture need to blend and elevate the space, without feeling too harsh or contrasting so it doesn't work with the flow. This is particularly important in a shipping container home where the space is limited, and you want to make sure everything blends effortlessly whether that is in terms of color or design. This doesn't necessarily mean that everything has to be of the same color, but things need to work well without any rooms or furniture sticking out like a sore thumb.

If you need help with this part, you can consult an interior designer. You could ask them what colors work well together and which don't, and how you can select shades that complement one another and make your place seem bigger and more spacious. If you want a DIY approach with adding color to your shipping container home, there are some resources that you can use to get the best results when it comes to coloring.

Online tools exist that can help you produce matching shades and mix and match others. You have software like Colormind, Adobe Color, Coolors, and Paletton. These tools basically all do the same thing, which is help you produce color combinations that work with your design and experiment with colors until you find what you are looking for. They have different user interfaces, but they all have the same function, more or else, and they're all free! So, experiment with those programs until you find the color combinations you need for your shipping container home.

You could also experiment with more than colors because who said you have to paint walls and be done with them? You could consider wallpaper that comes in different exciting and unique patterns and can give your place a unique style. Murals are also incredible, and they look majestic if you choose the right design. The point is, your choices are not limited, so take it slow and consider all your possible options from all angles.

Chapter 12: Sustainability Solutions

Interior design aside, you need to think about ways to improve your shipping container home's sustainability. One of the most important reasons many people invest in such homes in the first place is how they can be used to reduce carbon emissions of a residential home, not to mention live off the grid with minimal damage to the environment.

Contrary to popular belief, while container homes are better than traditional ones in terms of environmental friendliness, not all shipping container homes are necessarily eco-friendly. Your practices determine just how sustainable your shipping container home can be, and there are things that you will need to do to make sure that your shipping container home is environment friendly.

Appliances

Electrical appliances around the house are one of the areas in which you can seriously reduce the carbon footprint and minimize emissions. For starters, we leave a lot of devices on or on standby, which results in wasted electricity and all the harm that comes with that. It is obviously easier for us to leave devices on standby mode to turn on quickly, but it is wasteful. This is why a better approach would be turning these devices off when you are not using them, whether that is done through unplugging the machine or turning off switches.

You might think that standby devices don't necessarily consume too much power, but you would be mistaken. Studies show that at least 10% of residential electricity consumption is done through standby devices, which is huge. So, reducing energy consumption and being sustainable is definitely worth waiting a few extra seconds or even minutes until the device powers on.

Moreover, if sustainability is something you care about, you should also start considering investing in eco-friendly appliances, and there are many options. You can get an Energy Star-labeled refrigerator that minimizes electricity consumption in your shipping container home. You could also consider switching to a gas oven instead of an electricity-operated one, which would save you a lot of money on utility bills.

It would also be great if you replaced all your old appliances with new ones that run on more efficient systems that can reduce water and electricity consumption. Eventually, you will find that you not only created a much more sustainable living environment, but you also saved a lot of money because of those practices.

Use Sustainable Resources

The good news is there are always a lot of sustainable resources out there that you can use to make your shipping container home truly sustainable. The catch is, you might need to make a little more effort to find those resources, but the results are definitely worth it. You can start by using eco-friendly insulation. We talked earlier in the book about eco-friendly insulation like cork and wool or cotton, and you have other options like straw and hemp. Depending on your design and the climate in which you are building the shipping container home, it will be much better for the environment if you can use such materials for insulation.

Another resource you might change is your energy source. A solar panel system is ideal for a shipping container home living off the grid. You might pay a few thousand dollars to install the photovoltaic cells, but once that is completed, you will save a lot of money on energy bills in the long run. Solar energy is also one of the most eco-friendly solutions out there to generate electricity.

Recycle

Living in a shipping container home is sustainable in its own way, and if you want to really take things to the next level, consider recycling. This doesn't mean you should give away items to be recycled, you can do it at home. You should obviously have a garden around your shipping container home, and there is no better way to maintain that garden than using compost made out of everyday items we usually dispose of.

So, make a compost bin, in which you can make a compost pile to use in your garden. Things like fruit leftovers, vegetable peels, cotton clothes, tea bags, paper, and a lot more can be used in your compost as a way of recycling these items. When you recycle this much garbage you would usually throw away, it is much better for the environment. Such items would usually get tossed into a landfill, increasing the buildup of methane gas.

Grow Food

Picking up from the last point, and since you will be recycling your garbage, why not grow your own food? You already have a garden, so you absolutely can grow vegetables, and this practice can save a lot of carbon emissions. Plus, making your own food means you control what is added to the soil, so you know there are no added chemicals, and you get to enjoy organic and fresh vegetables.

Build Local

Some people often get dazed by the flash of imported building materials, but if you want to save money and reduce your carbon footprint, the best way to go is using local building materials. While it might always be an available option for everyone, definitely try to find local materials for your shipping container home. Some countries are rich in certain resources, while others might lack the same ones. So, dig a little, and if you find the building materials you need locally, get them. This will significantly lower your carbon footprint, not to mention save you shipping money.

Some people take things a step further and source materials that are not only local, but also surplus. If you look around in your area, you will probably find excess building materials and discarded raw materials that you can use, thus minimizing the need for buying new products. These materials might have some defects, but with a little effort, they can fit into your design and save you a lot of money because they are surplus.

There are many other things you can do for your shipping container home to make sure it is sustainable and poses minimal threat to the environment. From using energy-efficient light bulbs to water-efficient shower heads and toilets, the choice is yours. While these ideas will save you money in the long run, it is helping protect and save the environment that is the ultimate goal.

Chapter 13: Working on the Exterior

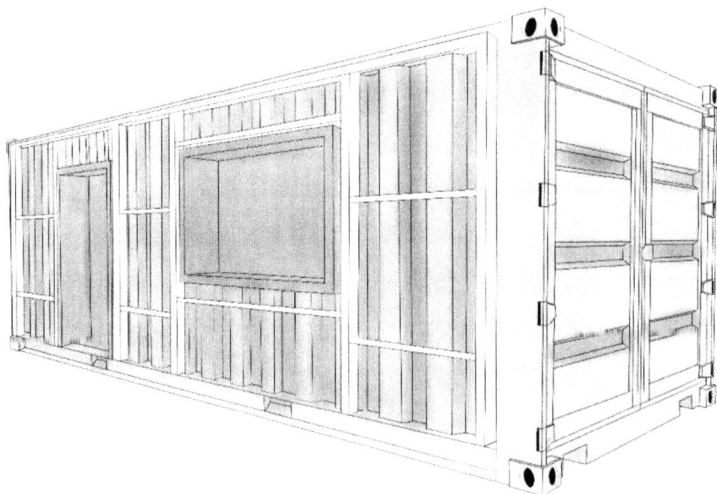

Installation base for the exterior part

We just about discussed everything related to your shipping container home's interior, from the finishing of the walls and floors to the furniture pieces you will get. Next, before we can wrap up the construction process, you will also have to finish the shipping containers' exterior. You have a lot of options here, like with most of the previous phases. One thing that will make a difference in this process is whether you have added exterior insulation to the shipping container. With insulation or not, you can work on giving the exterior of your home a beautiful finish that will impress visitors.

With Insulation

Having exterior insulation is always a good idea, as we have mentioned so often throughout the book. Fortunately, you have a some super options to finish the container's external walls if you have already added spray foam. You can paint over the insulation or add stucco to cover it. The important thing is to keep the insulation sealed and covered so it could be saved from direct sunlight and external conditions, which might compromise its integrity and cause its insulation to fail.

Painting: Painting is a great approach to finish your shipping container's external walls, but you must use specific kinds of paint. When painting over spray foam, you should either use water-based acrylic or latex paint, and avoid oil-based paint because it can damage the insulation. Also, steer clear from high-gloss paint since it will make any unevenness on the container pop's surface, unlike semigloss or flat paint, which can hide such inconsistencies and cover the insulation properly.

Before you start painting the container, inspect all the exterior walls of the shipping containers you will paint and look for rough edges or uneven parts. If you encounter those, use sandpaper to even them out so the paint will look smooth and uninterrupted on the exterior. Remember to always wear protective gear like goggles and masks to avoid inhaling fumes or having any particles enter your eyes.

After sanding the rough parts, you can start to paint the exterior surfaces of the shipping container. You need at least three coats of paint for the exterior surfaces, and you can choose whichever tool you prefer to disperse paint, whether it's a spray gun, brush, or roller. For the exterior, though, spray guns would be the best option since they give a consistent paint cover, and they are also the fastest to get the job done. If you're using one, make sure you try it out first on cardboard to know just how powerful the flow is. Rollers are good, too, but are slower than paint guns, while brushes are the slowest, but they give excellent control over the paint.

Some experts recommend applying a wax sealant over the paint once you're done painting. This will give the exterior surfaces of the shipping container a much better finish. Use several thin layers rather than one or two thick ones. Let each layer dry off first before applying the new one.

Stucco: Stuccoing the shipping container's exterior surfaces looks quite good and is one option to consider. However, if you're going to apply stucco, it is best that the spray foam has rough edges and finish so the stucco can latch on more easily. (This is one more thing to consider when making a decision on outside insulation.) A distinct advantage about stucco is that it is easy to deal with; you'll just purchase mixes that only need water added before being applied. Ask the salesperson about the surface area that can be covered by each bag of stucco mix.

Before you get to work, make sure you cover the ground around your shipping container home with a plastic sheet to protect it from any spills. To apply stucco, you first need to use adhesive to fix beading to the corners so that the beading is straight with no inconsistencies. Mix the stucco powder with water in a bucket and leave it for five minutes or so. Before you add the stucco, you need to make sure the external insulation surface is wet so that the material can grip onto the walls, using hose to water it down and keep it moist.

Then, using a steel trowel, work your way from the bottom of the shipping container wall to the top, applying the stucco as you go. Ensure that the stucco is applied evenly across the surface, using long strokes instead of short ones. The process of adding stucco needs to be done within half an hour of mixing, so make sure you are working within that time frame. In terms of layers, follow the same approach as you would with paint; apply several thin ones rather than a couple of thick ones. When the layer is still wet, rake each one after applying the stucco, which will provide a better grip for the next layer. For a more elegant finish to the stucco, you can finish the last layer with a polystyrene float.

Without Insulation

While exterior insulation is important and can help keep a lot of heat and cold out of your shipping container home, you can still skip it and focus on interior insulation. The plus side is your exterior will look like a shipping container home, which looks cool and adds to the uniqueness of the design and shows the true origins of the place you're living in.

Painting: If you're going to leave the exterior of your shipping container home exposed, *the least you should do* is paint it. An exterior without insulation looks good and shows the hard work you did to make this a home, but it also leaves the exterior exposed to elements. So, a layer of latex-based paint here can make a world of difference. The exterior would still look like a shipping container, but you will have provided a layer that can provide protection against rust and leakage.

Latex-based paint can improve the longevity of your shipping container home and keep the exterior looking nice, too. Before applying the paint, clean the surface of the shipping container, remove any stickers, and use sandpaper and grinders to get rid of rust that might be lingering on the exterior walls. Using a blade for this chore could prove tricky – and also dangerous. Remember to als0 cover the ground with plastic sheets before painting.

Experts recommend using alkyd enamel paint for the exterior of a shipping container, and you can apply it using brushes, roller, or spray guns. Like before, the spray gun is the fastest option with the most consistent cover, but you can also use the other two. Use also at least three layers of paint here on the exterior walls.

Timber Cladding

One more choice you have for finishing the exterior of your shipping container home is cladding it with timber. This is a great approach that will give your home a unique and beautiful finish, as well as the appearance of a wooden home. Timber cladding is also quite easy to fit, and it doesn't take up much time. Another advantage to this finish is that it provides an additional layer of protection to your shipping container home's exterior.

To start timber cladding your home, you need to start by fitting the battens on the exterior walls. Two by four-inch planks work great for timber cladding, but make sure they are fit to the container's size before you frame it. Put the battens at a spacing of 16 inches and fix them to the container. You can drill holes into the end of each batten at a distance of one foot from the roof and floor. Screw a bolt through the hole and tighten it to make sure it holds the batten properly. For vertical wood siding, you'll need to place the battens horizontally. For horizontal siding, you'll need to place the batten vertically.

Repeat the same process for each batten until they are tightly attached to the container from the top and bottom sides. Now that they surround the exterior of the shipping container, you can add the cladding. You simply get wooden boards and nail them to the exterior battens in a process similar to adding real wood to the interior, which we discussed earlier. Use stainless steel nails for nailing the boards so they can withstand the elements without rusting. Start at the bottom of the battens, make your way to the top, and make sure the cladding joints are overlapped.

After you add the timber cladding, treat it with a moisture- and UV-resistant coating to prolong the lifespan of the wood and help it withstand the sun's heat and moisture.

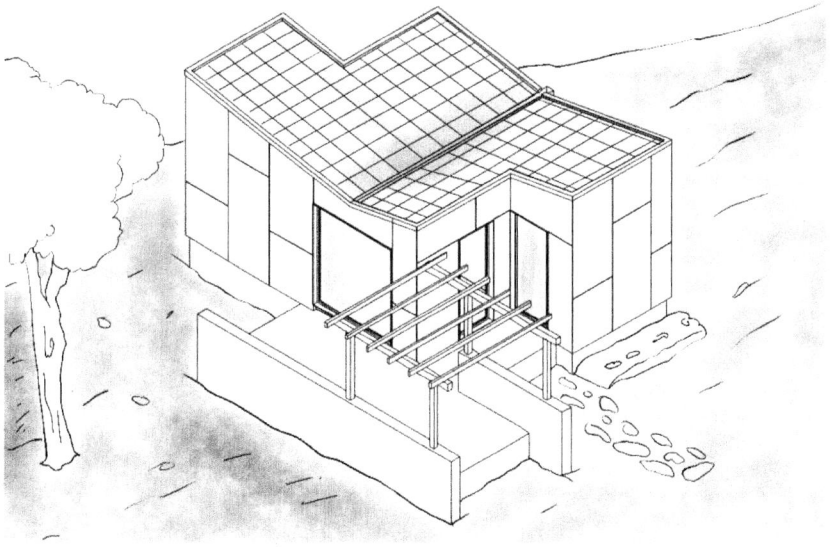

The container house, with all its accessories, roof, frames, and exterior decorations

Chapter 14: Security

The last thing we will be discussing in this book is the security of your home. Shipping containers are excellent structures that are durable and can last you for many years. They can withstand extreme conditions while sheltering you and keeping you safe. However, there is one thing we need to delve into as it is an essential part of any home - security.

One reason why many people are inclined to get a shipping container home is because they are secure. They are made of steel, so they appear that they are impenetrable with their heavy design and thick doors. Yet, know these heavy doors and overall sturdy design is not intended to keep intruders out, but to make sure the containers can survive long trips at sea or on trains.

Yes, a shipping container is considered safe, but it is not as safe as you might think, and it definitely isn't as safe as you would want your living space to be. This is why you need to make a few modifications and changes to ensure that they can be properly secured. In this next part, we will explore some things you can do to increase your shipping container home's security.

Why You Need Improved Security

Before you can start making changes to your home in terms of security, you must first understand what that means. When you plan this specific part ahead, it will help you move according to a solid plan and spend less money to secure your container home. For this part of the book, we will discuss physical security, keeping unwanted people from getting into your container. This is different from other security types like cybersecurity, which is not relevant to a shipping container home.

Reading all this, you might assume that you do not need additional security for your shipping container home, but that would be rolling the dice and hoping for the best, which is never a good idea. Think about it this way, do you have something to lose if someone breaks into your shipping container home? The answer would probably be yes. This isn't exactly an empty shipping container or one you're using to store junk. If that was the case, then there would be no need for further security. But this is a shipping container you have spent a lot of money to renovate and turn into a home, so you *do* have something to lose if someone breaks into it –and it is more than just the contents of your home.

There is valuable furniture, wiring, and personal belongings in your shipping container home, and those need to be kept safe at all times. It is not just the risk of theft that you should worry about, but also vandalism. There is always a chance that a disgruntled ex-employee, someone who doesn't like you - or even drug addicts - could break into your container home and smash everything you have worked so hard to build.

These points are especially important if you take where you live into consideration. Many people choose off the grid locations for their shipping container homes, so the possibilities of intruders increase in such cases. Most important, you need to be able to sleep at night without having to worry that it would be easy for any burglar to break into your home. Your family will occupy that living space, and you need to make sure they are kept safe.

Is It Worth the Cost?

If you have anything to lose by someone breaking into your shipping container home, then the answer is definitely yes, the extra security measures are worth the cost and effort. One of the most important roles that a security system plays in your home is deterrence, for starters. It scares away burglars and saboteurs. If they hear an alarm ring when they breach your home, they will most likely flee. Deterrence aside, a video surveillance system can help with finding the burglars and retrieving your stolen belongings.

You do need to understand the costs associated with security because there are a few, but as we mentioned, it is worth every penny considering you can keep property and lives safe. You have acquisition costs at first, which is the money you pay to buy whatever security measures you plan on using, whether that is an alarm system, a lock, or something else. Then you have operational costs because some measures will require regular work. Cameras and alarm systems will need monitoring. Systems might need batteries, and you will also need to invest in covering your security system up to look visually pleasing, so expect the need for paint and rust removal tools.

You will likely face replacement costs over time, opting for more robust systems or maintaining your current one. Consider acquisition and replacement in your security budget.

Security Measures for Shipping Container Homes

Now that we have discussed the importance of security measures for your new home and whether it would be worth the cost, it is time to explore some options you can add to your home to improve its security. There are specific measures you can follow for deterrence, prevention, and detection purposes, and you might get one or several of these depending on your judgment and budget. It is worth knowing these options so you can consider each while weighing the pros and cons.

Lights

Exterior lights are one of the best ways for deterring possible threats and risks to your shipping container home. Deterrence simply means making potential burglars or assailants believe that an attack on your property would be unsuccessful, so they won't even attempt it. Exterior lights are great for that purpose. Most attacks on property or people happen under the cover of the night, which is when it is least possible for intruders to get detected. Carefully placed lights around your container take away that advantage from potential intruders.

The best place to put exterior lights is on high ground, so it is difficult for anyone to tamper with them. You have quite a few options in terms of the lights themselves, from LED to halogen or even incandescent. LED lights are considered the best option, though, because they consume the least energy and they last the longest, making them the better investment. It is always a good idea to purchase decent lighting that will provide 360 degrees of coverage, ensuring there are no blind spots around your shipping container home from which burglars can penetrate.

The lights should also have a durable metal frame to survive the weather for a long time without you having to replace them every month or so. Avoid plastic light coverings; they won't last for long and they are not very reliable. There are other options with lights like motion-sensing lighting, which can save you a lot of power, but it doesn't provide as much deterrence as a regular light. In any case, you know the best light for the location you're in, so find a system that works well for your new home.

Warning Signs

One of the best deterrence approaches is putting up warning signs about your security system – even if you are bluffing. All you need is a little doubt and concern in a burglar's mind, which is usually enough to stop them. You can put up signs saying the entire property is watched and trespassers will be subject to the full extent of the law. Some people go the extra mile and even put up fake cameras, which come with the blinking lights and realistic design. This could also be enough to deter any possible home invasion.

Occupancy

No burglar wants to break into a house filled with people, so they often wait until they are certain that the place is empty and then break in. Your job is to make this complicated for them. You need to make it difficult for intruders to realize if there is someone at home or not. A clear and easy giveaway is where you park your car. If it is parked in the open, any burglar can easily identify it and realize there is no one at home. This is why it is always best to park your car in a closed garage that will let no intruders know if someone is home or not.

Another tactic that many people use is having electronic timers to set devices off, from TVs to radios. This will scare off any intruder near your home because they will think that someone is inside. Such systems are not as expensive as you might think, and many are easily activated via Wi-Fi. So, dig a little on the subject and decide what works best for your precious home

Clear the Area

The area around your shipping container home needs to be clear of any tools that might be used against you. Having bolt or wire cutters lying around is obviously a bad idea because anyone can use them to break into your place. Ensure that you have cleared the entire site of any tools you might have used in the construction process or other side projects.

Locks

Padlocks are one of the most important preventative measures you can take. Different types of padlocks can be used, but you need to think of them in the context of the rest of your shipping container home and how, where, and why you will be using them. When you buy a padlock, it has to be of the right size that needs to fit into whatever it is you will lock; consider the advantages of keyed locks versus combination locks.

1. Traditional Padlock

Traditional or conventional padlocks are the ones you see everywhere. They come in many materials and they all basically work the same way. One problem that conventional locks have is that the shackle is exposed, so it's easy to cut or grind off. You can get more expensive padlocks with shackles made of materials like hard boron carbide or other durable substances, and those are much more difficult to break into and intruders will be deterred if they meet up with such resistance.

Closed Shackle Padlock

This padlock is not very common, despite it being more secure than the previous example. A closed shackle padlock looks a lot like a conventional one, but the body of the lock covers most of the shackle. This definitely helps protect the lock from any tampering or break-in attempts, but it also reduces your space around the shackle, which makes it more difficult to handle.

2. Round-Shackle Padlock

Also known as disc padlocks, this one is circular and comes with a small and exposed shackle curved. Yet, unlike a conventional padlock, this one isn't spring-loaded; when you turn the key, the shackle moves out of the way as you do so. The design of a disc padlock is fairly simple, where two metal halves are often joined front to back. If you plan on getting this style of padlocks, invest in a high-quality model because, with the cheaper ones, the metal halves can be easily separated or even crushed.

3. Straight Shackle Padlock

Also known as shutter padlocks, this lock is often used with roll-up doors (also known as shutters) and provides excellent protection. The shackle is not curved or hooked but straight, which makes is highly resistant to tampering because if you think about it, this is a type of closed shackle lock.

Shutter locks are most commonly used with shipping containers, and a shutter lock might be the one recommended by the manufacturer. If you plan on getting one, make sure you are getting a high-quality lock made of hardened materials. Don't be tempted by imported types that look nice but are made of weak materials and easily tampered with. One of the best materials for shutter padlocks is brass covered in steel, which provides excellent protection and is highly durable.

It might be worth the investment to get a **padlock guard** for your shipping container home. It isn't a lock but a metal cover that encloses one of the mentioned types of padlocks, making them even more secure. In general, padlocks are cheaper than a lot of other options and types of locks, so if you add in a padlock guard, the cost might still be more affordable.

Before you get a padlock guard, make sure you have enough room for using the padlock itself because it might feel cramped. If you are good with metalwork, you can consider a DIY approach to making the guard since the design is pretty straightforward.

Fencing

There is nothing quite like a home situated in the open to encourage intruders to break into your place. No fence can possibly prevent any and every intruder, but it sure will make them think twice about breaking into your home. It will also significantly slow them down. You simply want to make the process of breaking into your home as complicated and exhausting as possible; a fence goes a long way in that regard.

You have a ton of options for your fence, depending on your budget. You can use anything from barbed wire or masonry to wood. There are quite a few things to consider before you decide or purchase one. Do you want the fence to block out the view into your home's exterior, or should it be see-through? What materials would cost you the least for the fence, especially if they're sourced locally from a nearby vendor?

There is also the DIY factor to consider. Some materials you can install on your own, but others will require contractors. Last but not least, you need to consider aesthetics. Will the fence's material and design complement your shipping container home, or will it stick out like a sore thumb? Also consider the surroundings as you decide; a barbed wire fence in a neighborhood with wooden fences might look out of place and ugly.

Doors: To make movement easier inside a shipping container home, some people might install personnel doors on the side of the shipping container, different from the end doors already installed in the container. Personnel doors might be a security threat since they are made of metal sheets with a core of foam or other materials, and sets of hinges like the ones you'd find on any door, though there are different ways to secure such a door.

1. Construction

To secure a door, the best time to start is during the construction process itself. A conventional door is basically two metal pieces with a core made out of a softer material between them. This is the general concept, but you can make a lot of changes, like altering the thickness of the metal pieces or adding metal reinforcement. If you need to look at models of secure doors, you needn't look further than fire-rated or hurricane-resistant doors since they are considered secure doors and will provide excellent protection against possible intruders.

Check the specifications of the door before buying it so you have a good idea of what the door is capable of and whether it can provide the desired protection. If money is not a problem, pricier options – like solid metal doors – can be as safe as a door can get.

Door Bar Lock

One of the easiest and fastest ways to ensure that your personnel door is secured is by adding a door bar lock. You will be adding a durable metal barrier in front of the door that can be swung aside when you don't need it. When you get a door bar, make sure the exterior hinge has unremovable pins so it can't be removed altogether. Also, remember that door bars don't cover the entire door, so this is not a reason to get a cheap door which makes it possible for an intruder to remove the door and find a way through.

Get or make a door bar that is sturdy and covers a good portion of the door, but don't make it too heavy because then it would be too difficult and annoying for you to regularly swing in and out of place. You should also include a built-in lockbox to keep the bar secured.

2. Hinges

Keeping a door secure is all about considering the hinges, especially the exterior hinges. Most shipping container homeowners would probably go with a door design that swings outward to save interior space already limited. However, doing so means you will need exterior hinges for the outward swing, and those hinges should have pins that cannot be removed. If you get cheap hinges with flaky pins, a burglar can easily unhinge the entire door and pull it out of its frame, and the lock you have on the door won't matter.

One of the best options for a solid hinge pin is the riveted pin. It comes with a unique thicker design and ensures that the pin is not attached to either side of the hinge. As a result, you get a secure design with a permanent hinge pin that cannot be removed. You can also go about it another way and install a hinge with a set screwed pin. With such hinges, the set screw doesn't allow the pin to be removed if the door is closed. If it is open, however, you can loosen the set screw and try to remove the pin.

Some people don't focus on pins, following a different approach. You can use door studs to keep your doors secured. If a burglar removed the pins from the hinges, a door stud can prevent the door from being pulled out of the frame. This works because you have small studs on the hinges' frame side, so they practically go into the door when closed and ensure it is secured. To go this way, you need to buy door hinges with studs built in to make your life easier.

3. Electronic Lock

An electronic lock might prove to be a good approach in certain cases. There are tons of different ways to keep your door secured, from using deadbolts to locking door handles, but they all work the same way, give or take a few minor differences. However, an electronic lock comes with a few advantages, especially if the container is inhabited or used by quite a few people. You can set it to include different password combinations, so there will be no need to distribute a lot of keys that might easily get lost and cause problems. Some newer models can be operated via Wi-Fi and you can unlock them remotely – a very cool and useful feature!

No matter which approach you choose for securing your doors, this is one area of your design process you need to carefully consider. Ensuring that your shipping container entrances are secured is the best way possible to prevent any intruders from breaking into your place and stealing or wreaking havoc. Give this consideration much time and attention.

Windows

While doors might present a security threat sometimes, that is nothing compared to windows. They can be so risky that some shipping container homeowners don't even use windows, but that is not common. Most shipping container homes have quite a few windows in the design, and they do make the place look and function a lot better. The challenge is trying to make sure the windows are as secure as possible.

A window is usually the least secure part of your shipping container home, and burglars can easily find their way into your home if they break the glass. So, external security around your windows is definitely a good idea, and you have a lot of options here.

Covers

Like door bar locks, a window cover can protect the windows in your shipping container home. The difference between the cover and the door bar lock is that the former is solid metal, considering how less secure windows are compared to doors. The great thing about this option is that it is not permanent, and you can keep it open when you want to. It can swing vertically or horizontally, and there are even barn door designs, which is a horizontal slide. Choosing one of these options won't depend on just your preferences, but also the design of your shipping container home, which might require choosing a specific one that suits its design.

For instance, vertical swinging covers require permanent hinge pins. The vertical swinging cover is one of the better options, generally, because as it rolls up, it provides shade and reduces the direct sunlight falling on your window. Like with door bar locks, you should use a lockbox on the window covers, too.

Bars/Mesh

Probably the safest way to keep the exterior of your shipping container home safe is to install steel bars or mesh. The problem with this option is that these are pretty permanent solutions so you can't remove them at will, and they might make you feel trapped inside your own home. That is not even the worst part; steel mesh or bars seriously hinder the vision out of the container, which is not good, especially if you live in a place surrounded by greenery or beautiful scenery.

On the other hand, these options provide the best security and ensure that it will be difficult for an intruder to break into your shipping container home. Metal bars are the better choice, though, because the steel with an expanded mesh is thinner, so it might provide less protection.

Detection

We talked earlier about deterrence and prevention techniques to both deter and prevent intruders from getting into our shipping container home. Now, we will discuss some detection techniques that can help you detect any intruders who might ignore the deterrence elements and wander into the vicinity of your home. Detection is your last line of defense, and the point is to have a solid system in place that can detect any invasion and generate a proper response.

1. Alarms

An alarm system is one of the better detection techniques out there, and it also works for deterrence. A well-placed system can detect intruders and possible attempts at break-in, especially if you are not at home. As it does so, it will notify the homeowner and trigger a police response, with some systems at least.

Alarm systems rely on a variety of sensors, and this includes motion, heat, and sound sensors, and other types that vary with the system. If the sensors are triggered and they detect something is wrong, a response is triggered. It can be a loud alarm sound or notifying a security company or the police, while some trigger a phone call or text message to the homeowner. Either the loud noise will scare intruders, or your system will send a silent alarm to law enforcement so they can capture the intruder before they leave.

Invest in an alarm system with a battery backup, which is crucial if the intruder is smart enough to cut off the electrical power supply powering the alarm system. You don't need a sophisticated alarm system for your new home; after all, it's not a bank! A basic system of windows and door sensors and a motion detector would do the trick and can provide the security you need. You can get a more advanced system with more sensors and options if money is not a problem, but it might be overkill.

2. Dogs

It might sound old fashioned in the high tech world we live in, but a security dog is one of the best deterrence, prevention, and detection techniques out there that can keep your home secure. A dog can stop or attack any intruder trying to break into your home, and they can be efficient at making them flee. A dog's bark also provides an excellent detection technique because they are mostly trained to bark at unwanted intruders. A lot of factors play into your choice of security dog, but a strong enough breed can be an excellent protector for you and your family, plus your belongings.

3. Cameras

We mentioned fake cameras before as a means of deterrence, but these are the real deal. You have two options with security cameras. It is a live one that transmits the video feed elsewhere, and those are usually connected to an alarm system. You can install outdoor and/or indoor live security camera models, but for security, the exterior one should be more than enough. The problem with that is you might need more than one security camera on the outside to cover the entire perimeter of your shipping container home. You will also have to pay a monthly monitoring fee because there has to be someone keeping an eye on that security feed.

The second option you have is the record for later cameras, which don't transmit live feed anywhere but rather record the events for later viewing and identification of the intruders. Unlike live cameras, you don't need an internet connection for these cameras. You also need not pay the monthly monitoring fee.

FAQ – Top 10 Most Common Questions

1. Which US states allow shipping container homes?

Most US states allow shipping container homes, though the regulations may vary. You should check the rules and regulations of the state before you plan for your shipping container home.

2. Which countries allow shipping container homes?

As of today, the US and Canada are the biggest countries in North America that allow for shipping container homes. As for Europe, many European countries have also legalized shipping container homes like France, the UK, Belgium, Austria, Germany, and Spain. You should, however, always check first or consult with a legal professional before going forward.

3. Are shipping container homes safe?

To put it shortly, yes, shipping container homes are safe. They are made of corrugated steel and they are durable since they are designed to withstand long trips in the sea or on trains, so they are quite durable.

4. Are shipping container homes cheaper than the average traditional house?

Yes, they are. However, depending on your budget, you can make a shipping container home almost as expensive as a traditional house. Fortunately, you can make one for a fraction of the cost, too.

5. Can a shipping container home have a basement?

Depending on your initial design, you can make room for a basement or a sub-floor to be used as a garage, yes.

6. Can shipping container homes be moved?

Yes, they can, and this gives them another edge over a traditional house, which can never be moved.

7. Do you have to pay property tax for shipping container homes?

If you want your shipping container home to be considered as a piece of real estate (meaning it qualifies for mortgages and can be used as collateral), then you will need to pay property tax.

8. How much does an average shipping container home cost?

On average, a shipping container can cost between $60,000 and $80,000. However, you can make a more affordable shipping container home for as low as $20,000.

9. Should you build it yourself or hire contractors?

This will depend on several factors, starting with your budget. You can do it yourself, but you must check a detailed guide, like the one in this book, on how to move forward. If, however, you are not so handy or don't want a DIY approach, then you can use contractors.

10. How long can a shipping container home last?

The average shipping container home can last you up to 25 years without complications. If you regularly maintain it, though, and handle any rust or leakage problems promptly, then it could last much longer.

Conclusion

We have covered pretty much everything you need to know to make your shipping container a home. Whether you're going to DIY or enlist contractors' help, we've gone over everything you need to make this work. Proceeding on a tight budget would be best for DIY, and the great thing about this project is that you *can* do it yourself. It is not a walk in the park, and it will take a lot of planning and effort on your side, but the outcome will certainly be worth it.

If you follow the tips and guidelines mentioned in this book, with a DIY approach, you can build a shipping container home for a budget of anything between $20,000 and $30,000 if you are mindful of the resources and working to save money. If you are less than efficient, the cost can go up to $50,000, which is still great and cheap if you compare this to a traditional home.

Remember that you have different options for every step of this project, which is one reason why it is so great! You are building your own home, so there are no limitations as to what you can do. This is a very fulfilling and satisfying project, and the outcome will be the place you get to live in. So, take your time planning this thoroughly and consider all possible angles more than once. You can walk away with a beautifully designed home that can last you for years, and more important, you can pass it on to your children with little maintenance.

There is a reason shipping containers home are popular now, and why they are a significant part of the future of residential properties. You can customize the home of your dreams for a fraction of the budget of building a traditional home. Plus, you get to see it being built from scratch, which is extremely gratifying, especially if you are the one doing it yourself. Moreover, even if it wasn't an original goal, you'd be building an eco-friendly home made out of sustainable materials and is infinitely better for the environment than a traditional house.

Last, a shipping container home is great to be self-sufficient. You can live off the grid with your own source of power and your own garden where you plant what you eat. A shipping container home might just be your way into a less stressful and more peaceful life. So, enjoy making it, because you will certainly enjoy living in it.

References

4 Ways to Insulate a Container Home. (2018, April 24). Rise.

Alex. (2019, August 30). *How Does Container Home Electrical Work?* SimpleTerra. https://www.simpleterra.com/how-does-container-home-electrical-work/

Best Ways to Insulate Shipping Containers. (2015, March 23). Discover Containers. https://www.discovercontainers.com/5-methods-to-insulate-your-shipping-container-home/

Cleaning Your Shipping Container Before Use. (2018, August 14). Land, Sea, & Air Shipping Services - InterlogUSA. https://www.interlogusa.com/answers/blog/cleaning-your-shipping-container-before-use/

Container Homes - Pros, Cons & Cost Comparison. (2018, November 29). Rise.

Design a Container House. (n.d.). DiscoverDesign.

Do You Need a Permit for Shipping Containers? | Sigma Container Corporation. (2019, December 23). New & Used Shipping Containers. https://www.sigmacontainer.ca/blog/do-you-need-a-permit-for-shipping-containers/

Home. (n.d.). Discover Containers. https://www.discovercontainers.com/

Home, I. C. (2020, March 1). *Electrical Wiring of Shipping Container Home.* IContainerHome.Com.

https://icontainerhome.com/electrical-wiring-of-shipping-container-home/

How to add Plumbing to a Cargo Container | eHow.com. (2020). EHow.Com. https://www.ehow.com/how_4485929_add-plumbing-cargo-container.html

How to Choose the Right Shipping Containers. (n.d.). Discover Containers. https://www.discovercontainers.com/complete-guide-to-buying-shipping-containers/

INSULATION RECOMMENDATIONS A Quick Guide to Cost, Health, and Environmental Considerations. (n.d.).

serrajr. (2019, June 25). *5 Reasons to Buy a Container Home.* ECONTAINERS. https://www.econtainersmod.com/5-reasons-to-buy-a-container-home/

Shipping Container Conditions explained | WWT, CW, As-is. (2019, February 28). Container XChange. https://container-xchange.com/blog/container-conditions-and-grading-explained/

Shipping Container Homes: A 2019 Guide to Buying & Building Container Houses. (2019, July 2). Stackhouse Container Homes. https://stackhousecontainerhomes.com/shipping-container-homes-a-2019-guide-to-buying-building-container-houses/

Shipping Container Zoning, Permits, and Building Codes. (2019, August 27). Discover Containers. https://www.discovercontainers.com/shipping-container-zoning-permits-and-building-codes-which-states-allow-them/

Should You Build Your Own Container Home? (n.d.). Discover Containers. https://www.discovercontainers.com/should-you-build-your-own-shipping-container-home/

Smita. (2019, August 22). *7 Benefits of Shipping Container Home Design.* Marine Insight. https://www.marineinsight.com/recreation/7-benefits-of-shipping-container-home-design/

Printed in Great Britain
by Amazon